At the End of the Road

REFLECTIONS ON LIFE IN AN ADIRONDACK VALLEY

Ruth Mary Lamb

Pyramid Publishing Inc.
Utica, New York

ISBN-10 1-886166-12-9
ISBN-13 978-1-886166-12-7

Some of the essays, in part or in different form, have appeared in other publications:
Adirondack Life: "Rookery of the Year", August 1994, "One Dam Thing After Another", August 1996, "Off the Grid", September 2000; *New England Writers' Network*: "Recycling", Spring 1999; *Glens Falls Post Star*: "Maple Fever", Spring 1997, vol. 4 #2; *Lake George Mirror*: "Notes of an Adirondack Valley Watcher", August 8 & 15, 2003, "Maple Fever", Summer 2001.

Grateful acknowledgement is made for permission to quote from the following:
Stirring the Mud by Barbara Hurd © 2001 Barbara Hurd, (permission, Beacon Press); "The Ultimate Canvas" by Gary Kowalski © 2003, (permission, Gary Kowalski; reprinted July/August 2003, *U.U. World*; originally excerpted from *Science and the Search for God*, Lantern Books, 2003); *Everyday Blessings* by John Kabat-Zinn and Myla Kabat-Zinn © 1997 Myla Kabat-Zinn and Jon Kabat-Zinn (permission, Hyperion; All rights reserved); *River Walking: Reflections on Moving Water* by Kathleen Dean Moore © 1995 Kathleen Dean Moore (permission, Lyons and Buford); *The Humanure Handbook* by J. C. Jenkins © 1994 J.C. Jenkins (permission, Joseph Jenkins).

The cover painting, *Beaver Wetland and Catamount Mt.* was painted in 2005 for this book by artist Nancy Rogal, of Bolton Landing, New York and West Chester, Pennsylvania. Chapter illustrations were created in 2007 by Sally Strasser of Glens Falls, New York.

Pyramid Publishing Inc.
PO Box 8339
Utica, New York 13505

www.pyramidpublishingservices.com

To Sandy

Cover Artist Nancy Rogal

Nancy Dalton Rogal's family has been on Lake George for six generations. Growing up in Schenectady, majoring in art at Skidmore, she has spent a lifetime of vacations, and now retirement, painting the Lake and unspoiled wild places. She and her husband Bill renovated her Grandmother's house on North West Bay, and she is active in four conservation groups, as well as Bolton's Lake Shore Gallery.

Chapter Illustrator Sally Strasser

Sally lives in Glens Falls, New York, where she runs her decorative arts contracting business. She is a Fine Arts graduate of Williams College and holds a Masters Degree in painting from Bennington College. Her favorite subjects are skies, forests, and fields.

Contents

Acknowledgements

This book would not have happened without the loving support of my family. My husband Sandy was indispensable. My daughter Bonnie, and two sons Glenn and Bruce, and their wives Sue and Samia, encouraged me and gave me the courage to keep writing. My sister-in-law Kitty got us started on our adventure, and in sharing her memories helped give me a richer picture of Journey's End.

Successful writers who shared their craft, helping me to improve my writing, include Jennifer Sahn of *Orion Magazine*, Le Anne Schreiber at the New York State Writers Institute, and Annick Smith at Recursos de Santa Fe Writing Yourself Workshop. I am particularly indebted to Linda Hasselstrom's critiques when she worked with me in the Split Rock Online Mentoring program.

I cherish the patient reviewers who read the entire manuscript and shared ideas for improving its language, grammar, and organization. Thanks to David and Pat Martin, Jean Hoefer, Margo Burrell, Kay Hafner, Pat McGivern, Milton Wright, Nancy King Smith, Kathy Conerty, and Judy Coburn. My non-fiction writing group friends gave me caring comments, spread over many months: Greta Eichel, Marilyn Sandberg, Alice Zeiger, and Judy Coburn.

Special thanks to Neal Burdick for writing the introduction. I am indebted to Nancy Rogal who painted *Beaver Wetland and Catamount Mt.* for the cover, and Sally Strasser who created the chapter drawings.

Introduction

What is it that causes some of us to throw off the comforts of suburbia and literally head for the hills, beyond the end of the road, off the grid? What atavistic urges compel us to revert to the ways of our forebears, to throw generally accepted notions of progress into reverse and march steadily, steadfastly backward?

Ruth Lamb implicitly asks and in large measure explicitly answers these questions in this memoir of her and her husband's move from Boston's cultured environs to a rundown farmhouse at the end of a dirt road in a mostly abandoned valley "up back of" Lake George, as the locals might put it, in just about the most middle of nowhere that one can get in the Northeast anymore.

The modest house, a family place (which may in part explain the compulsion to return to it) is aptly named Journey's End, though we quickly realize the journey is not merely physical, and the part that isn't physical doesn't end, doesn't march backward, but goes on in joy and sorrow like the faithful turnings of the seasons. Its accessories include "160 acres of fields, wetlands and hilly forests," mostly encircled by Adirondack Forest Preserve lands, public lands, gloriously undeveloped. "Beyond the house," Ruth says, "Wardboro Road peter(s) out." So has Wardboro, the scattering of farms and homes, schools and sawmills that made this valley a thriving, vibrant community until the forces of economic, social migration and state politics drove people away as surely as the spring freshet that nearly persuaded Ruth and Sandy to stay away. They would be "the only year-round human residents" of the valley. "Ours was a reverse migration," Ruth writes early on, though we soon come to see that in many ways it is not a reverse at all but rather an advance toward new understandings.

If they sought problems to solve, it quickly becomes clear that they did the right thing. And if they wanted to observe fauna and flora, they came to the right place. As for living simply, well, sometimes that can get very complicated. Take, for example, the phone matter. One day, when Ruth realizes she could chop her foot with an axe, isolation suddenly takes on a less appealing specter. So in comes a cell phone, into this hollow walled by mountains, and it has to be rigged so as to cause the truck's horn to blow when someone tries to call. And they must drive around to find a spot where they can connect an outbound call, not a good use of time if you've taken an axe to your foot. What was that about simple living?

As for how they figured out bathing, you'll have to read that for yourself. First, though, try to imagine how you would arrange to take a bath in a place that doesn't have much in the way of serviceable plumbing. Or how to do word processing where there's no electricity to power a computer.

But along with the technical difficulties come the serene pleasures of getting to know, and lightly become one with, their adopted ecosystem. Black flies, bats and garter snakes are their hosts, and they try to be gentle newcomers. "We work our way slowly through the obstacles," Ruth writes, "but also let our senses overload on mountains, woods, rushing streams, bird song, and summer's tranquil times." The chilling fact that winter lurks just beyond the northern hills, preparing to plow down upon them, does not frighten but invigorates them with the anticipation of new adventures, new footprints, new problems to solve.

And when winter ends, the problems don't. Here's just one: what to do when deer wipe out the apple saplings, strawberries, cabbages, broccoli and Brussels sprouts. Well, who's the intruder here? Sometimes you just have to accommodate and compromise. And then there are the chipmunks—it is indeed a miracle of nature how such little creatures can have such a big impact. They're like snow in a way: one flake doesn't do much, but combine it with hordes of others and you have…a problem. As with the myriad other dilemmas the Lambs face trying to live simply, though, they eventually figure out how to make a go of the gardens, enough to become nearly self-sustaining.

With all this wildlife, it's hard for the Lambs to think of themselves as isolated. And indeed they are not, as they move toward acceptance that the bugs, birds and beasts are a part of their lives now, not apart from them. And they welcome their association with their seasonal human neighbors, who provide support and "how to" knowledge, much as transpired in days long past. They even learn to tolerate, though they grit their teeth and practice forbearance, the hunters, snowmobilers and off-roaders.

There is much joy in their education—exploring the mountains that embrace them, even getting lost (or perhaps, like Daniel Boone, merely bewildered) briefly; watching the seasons go round and round; learning when the wildflowers will come again and how they live; discovering, always discovering. And as it always is close to nature, there's tragedy too. When their beloved cat becomes a midnight meal for an owl, Ruth is forced to call out her fears of her own certain demise, but also to comprehend that all of nature is one.

This is not all mushy nature-loving writing, though. There is much fond and fine description of sunsets and chrysalises and marsh marigolds and toads and such, but if you're squeamish, skip the parts about what they learned from their own excrement. Ruth has a literary bent; Emerson and Thoreau make cameos, but only where they fit and the rest of the time they stay in the wings, while the excerpts from her journals demonstrate that she has her own acquired and lovingly polished skills at observing nature affectionately but frankly and at converting those observations into words that can tug at us, enlighten us, place us in Wardboro Valley with her. It's pleasant there, all in all, and Ruth Lamb a delightful, honest guide; turn the page and let her take you in.

—Neal Burdick

North Country native Neal Burdick is the editor of the Adirondack Mountain Club's magazine, *Adirondac*, and of its Forest Preserve series of guidebooks, as well as a regular contributor to *Adirondack Explorer*. The co-editor of the anthology *Living North Country* (North Country Books, 2001), he lives in Canton, where his day job is publications editor at St. Lawrence University.

Things in the margins, including humans who wander there,
are often on the brink of becoming something else, or someone else...

Barbara Hurd, *Stirring the Mud: On Swamps, Bogs and Human Imagination*

Journey's End

In my mind's eye, I see Journey's End as it was in 1986, the year my mother-in-law Helen died. The decaying farmhouse sat at the end of the road in a wild Adirondack valley, forgotten. I would never have predicted then that in the coming years this place would transform our lives.

The green-shingled farmhouse sat silent in the June sunshine. Wasps slipped into and out of nests they were crafting beneath roof slates. Heavy wood shutters barred the front door and the six first-floor windows, leaving the two downstairs rooms as dark as night. A mouse scrambled up the inside of the fieldstone cellar wall and slipped into the kitchen through a crack under the door. It didn't need any light to find its way across the eight-inch-wide unpainted floorboards into the cobwebby living room. It was squeaking as it ran up one of the legs of a metal frame bed and burrowed into remnants of a mattress where its babies awaited. Bats slept upstairs, attached to wall boards, whose cracks allowed them to fly outside at night to feed above Flybrook's beaver meadows.

Blackberries grew in a tangle, hiding the decrepit woodshed that enclosed the back door. The brambles had taken over the backyard and spread along the north side of the house, too. Their thorny branches hid shards of china dishes and abandoned bottles that former inhabitants had tossed out the door. Only my father-in-law Carl had cared enough about this last Wardboro Valley farmhouse to keep its yard and fields mowed. And he had died three years before.

He loved this place. Whenever he could, he drove the eleven miles from his home in Bolton Landing to spend a few hours mowing the old farm fields where his mother had lived as a small child. We think it was called Journey's End even when she toddled around the yard. I can picture Carl sitting in a rocking chair on the front porch, smoking a cigar. My husband Sandy recalls good times as a young teen clearing brush with his dad, followed by hours of chopping firewood. They got along best when they just worked next to each other. When they opened their mouths, they didn't agree on much. Only the family men went on these expeditions. Sandy's sister Kitty and his mother Helen were not included.

Helen's death on January 12, 1986, seemed so senseless. This vital woman, who worked for years as a guidance counselor helping the younger generation find themselves, had given up on life. Cigarettes, beer, and hoarded pills were the weapons she used against herself. Sandy in Massachusetts and Kitty in California tried to intervene, but were helpless against her determination.

In June we gathered at her home near Lake George. Kitty and her husband Ed traveled east in their RV, which they parked in Helen's driveway. Kitty's daughters journeyed from California and Ohio, while Sandy and I and two of our three grown children drove west from Boston. Together we cleared out fifty years of living, cried a little, and put the Bolton Landing house up for sale.

Co-owners now, Sandy and Kitty decided to keep Journey's End. The old farmhouse came with 160 acres of fields, wetlands, and hilly forests tucked into Lake George's western watershed, three and one-half miles from the main road. The dozen farms that had spread their fields along Valley roads were mostly sold to New York State around 1920. Only seven pockets of private land existed along this stretch of dirt road, all surrounded by Adirondack Forest Preserve lands—forever wild. Beyond the house, Wardboro Road petered out. Its unmaintained extension wandered for five miles to the next macadam road, where a sign proclaimed: *Flybrook Road, Closed for Mud Season.*

Following the gathering, we returned to Wayland, Massachusetts, to our normal lives. We had an empty nest, for our three children Bonnie, Glenn, and Bruce, had all gone off to college. I was a student, as well. I flooded the house with textbooks as I, who had nearly flunked college chemistry years ago, took the undergraduate science courses needed for a degree in nutrition. I enjoyed being a student so much that I then set out to get a second degree in public health. I also worked part-time nutrition jobs at a neighborhood health center in South Boston and at the Natick Visiting Nurses. I was busy.

So was Sandy. His commute to Boston, where he oversaw the Health Department, started pre-dawn. After strapping on his backpack, he let himself quietly out of the house and ran four miles in his jogging shoes to a suburban mall where he caught the bus. In Boston he ran to City Hospital where he dealt with worrisome infant death rates, lead poisoning of children, and growing rates of AIDS infections. He also taught pediatrics and infectious disease epidemiology at Boston University. AIDS, however, which at that time was untreatable, had taken over his life.

It seemed he never had enough time to deal with all the death that veiled his working hours. He met with legislators, the mayor, city councilmen, and AIDS Action Committee members to seek solutions to this public health emergency. He found himself on a political hot seat when he struggled to implement a needle exchange program to protect drug addicts, who were spreading AIDS by sharing contaminated needles. While Boston's Mayor Flynn supported him, Massachusetts Governor Dukakis refused to allow passage of the proposal.

The death of Bob Sappenfield, a young AIDS activist, shocked us. I usually avoided funerals. They stirred up powerful feelings that scared me. Since it seemed important to honor this dedicated man, I joined Sandy at the memorial service Bob wrote before he died. His words moved us deeply.

"You, too, are dying but you don't know when. Use your remaining days in ways that are truly important to you." Many an evening after that, we talked together about what we wanted to do with the rest of our lives.

In the meantime, Kitty and Ed parked their RV at Journey's End for the summer and started cleaning out the old house. Out came rotten hotdogs that had been stored in an old fashioned icebox in the shed, cobwebs, mouse turds, the resident bats, stinky, mouse-chewed mattresses, and broken furniture. Once they dug up the blackberry bushes for gardens, they unearthed the shards of broken dishes and discovered the fascinating collection of old bottles. When we arrived to help on a weekend in late summer, we found them hard at work. I admired their tenacity.

I remembered that when our kids were adolescents and we came to visit Sandy's parents, we chose to stay away from Carl's dirty, unkempt place in the woods. Instead, we camped on Lake George islands during most summer vacations. The one year Sandy led the kids on a hike to Journey's End they tried to follow abandoned Flybrook Road. Carl dropped them off at the "road closed for mud season" sign and they set off. Unfortunately, the road divided into so many logging tracks they never got to Wardboro Valley. Fortunately, they did find an inhabited house where they called for a ride back to town.

That first summer, Kitty and Ed tackled the shabby house. Wielding paint brushes and hammers, they brightened the dark, dingy rooms with white paint on the walls and maroon on the unfinished floors. Ed built a new two-seater outhouse, using a generator powered by the RV to saw boards. After driving the two hundred miles from Massachusetts to spend a few weekends helping, we realized their efforts were slowly turning the dumpy old place into a magnet for us. Dreaming of a well, we all dug around a wet spot in the wooded hillside above the house. After cracking off chunks of ledge and lifting them out of the ground, we created a rocky hole into which water seeped and collected. I eyed it, wondering what we had started.

During the next three summers Kitty and Ed persisted. They RV'd back from their winter adventures and dug into projects at Journey's End. Ed built a new shed and a screened porch. The seep in the woods became a spring-fed well after they implanted a large culvert as a collector and packed clay around it. Ed imagined tying it to the house by black PVC pipe laid atop the ground. When they found a discarded kitchen sink storage unit, they hustled the treasure back to Journey's End. Once a pipe was connected to both the well and the house, water gurgled downhill, pouring out of the faucet on demand. We were so excited you would have thought we had won the lottery.

The more we helped, the more we felt at home. We envied all the time Kitty and Ed spent in the Valley. Back in Massachusetts I now worked in Wayland's town center, sometimes bicycling to the job I shared with another woman. We supervised the local senior center; her specialty, music; mine, food. I liked my part-time position, but found myself working many extra hours.

Sandy was drained by his whirlwind career in urban public health. It seemed he never had time to do anything else. Then there was the cancer. When he had an innocent looking growth on the side of his face biopsied, it proved to be a basal cell carcinoma. His mortality loomed. We talked more seriously about the future.

That summer Kitty told us they were through with roaming and were planning to settle in New Mexico. We quickly sorted out what was important. We wanted to retire early while we still had the energy, and pioneer in Wardboro Valley. I hoped that living at Journey's End would allow us to immerse ourselves in a wild place, becoming part of the network of creatures already there. Our savings, added to a small inheritance left by Sandy's mother, would help underwrite this experiment. I envisioned us as observers who slipped out of the old farmhouse to spy on non-human neighbors.

I will never forget the mild March day in 1990 when we made that first spring journey to take our turn as Valley caretakers. We left the hyacinths, daffodils, and tulips in our Wayland yard, threw belongings into a bag, grabbed Malta, our orange cat, and hurried off in our new 4 x 4 Ford truck. As we sped northward, along the New York State Northway, the cat asleep in my lap, we watched the countryside edge back toward winter. The radio warned this cloudy day could erupt with heavy showers, with possible flooding. "Do you suppose our road will flood?" I asked. Sandy shrugged.

Snow covered the ground as we eased off the Northway onto Route 9N. This road would take us north, just west of Lake George. Today its clear waters lay hidden under snow-covered ice. The white-shrouded mountains surrounding the lake loomed eerily, there one minute and gone the next in swirling clouds and fog. Hurrying through deserted resort towns, we homed in on the increasingly rough forest lying northwest. Eight miles beyond the last town, we arrived at the turn-off.

With the first jolts of the dirt road, Malta stretched and investigated, staring out the window, tail twitching. About the same time, rain began to patter around us. I, too, stared. Just to the right, Northwest Bay Brook, already swollen with snow melt, charged along almost above its banks. I knew Sandy relished this adventure, but I wondered what we were getting into. He piloted the truck across the Alma Farm Flats, where the road and rocky brook coexist at about the same level. Today they commingled. The shallow water sloshed under us, as Sandy drove slowly along. Then the brook went its way, and we went ours. I unclenched my fists when we made the next stream crossing on the sturdy bridge that many years ago had replaced a ford.

Padanarum Road continued straight ahead. We turned right onto Wardboro Road. I held my breath, hoping our new truck could tackle whatever lay before us. Malta had seen enough. She again curled into a lump in my lap. Even though the plowed surface ended abruptly, the truck moved obligingly through the half-foot of snow until we crested a rise. To my right the land dropped about thirty feet to the stream below. Ahead, the road disappeared into a mix of glare ice and deep slush. I tried not to notice how close we were to the edge of the narrow road where the land disappeared. The rain drummed insistently. We looked at each other.

"Keep going?" asked Sandy.

"What will we do about Malta if we get stuck?" I worried, staring at the pelting rain. "It's not as if we brought enough supplies to get marooned at Journey's End. But how can we turn around? We just got here!"

Sandy sat thoughtfully, "Well, let's check out the other end of Padanarum Road and see if we can go that way to the Northway. If that road's open, let's stay."

So he carefully backed up the truck, while I closed my eyes, terrified the tires would slip sideways, carrying us like a boulder down into the stream. Once we reached level ground, he turned the truck around, and we set off to explore the rest of Padanarum Road. If it wouldn't let us pass, we'd have to leave, splashing back through the flooding road. After crossing a side-stream bridge, the road went vertical, heading for the sky. My body tensed as the truck (with its windshield wipers working fiercely) lurched up this long hill. Then we saw it—a deep gully crossing the road. A washout! Disappointment mingled with relief as Sandy cautiously backed the truck down the hill. We admitted defeat.

During that long drive back to Massachusetts the truck cab reverberated with Malta's purrs and our unspoken worries about the practical realities of coming to live in this wild place. I loved living a ridge away from the Sudbury River in Massachusetts. I could walk out my back door in summer and ski during snowy winters, following paths that led through woodlands or to the river marshlands. If I stood quietly, consorting Canada geese, floating wood ducks, and paddling muskrats might show up. But my busy life interfered, and I hardly ever trekked there. I had hoped that in Wardboro Valley my life would be centered in the network of creatures and plants. Now it seemed the Valley was sending us a message. Stay away!

We didn't want to stay away. We wanted at least a trial year at Journey's End, where we could grow our own vegetables. The tall oak trees on our small Wayland lot discouraged gardening. We did plant a plot in a community garden along the river, but we fought woodchucks there and despaired of harvesting much of anything.

We wanted to become less dependent on nonrenewable fuels for heating. While we had shifted to partly heating our Wayland house with an All Nighter energy-efficient wood stove, at Journey's End an endless supply of wood awaited us. To find firewood, Sandy would no longer have to visit state forests that had tree thinning programs, toting his new Sears chainsaw. He would just go out the back door.

After we were turned back that March day, we persevered, leaving our jobs, and scurrying around getting ready for what we hoped would be our successful migration from the Sudbury River Valley to Wardboro Valley…and Journey's End. In this old farm we hoped not to end, but to start, a journey into adventurous retirement.

On Friday, April 13, we returned. The truck was stuffed: a chain saw, shovels, All Nighter woodstove, new futon and mattress, Carl's recliner chair, suitcases, and boxes stuffed with t-shirts, jeans, underwear, sweaters, jackets, sheets, towels, blankets, favorite cookbooks, special pots and pans, Helen's sterling silverware, important papers, backpacks, hiking boots, sleeping bags, and groceries we hoped would last for at least a couple of weeks. On top, lay a thirty-foot metal extension ladder. We were prepared to stay.

By then, the floods were gone, mud season was over, and Padanarum Road extended its welcome mat. Leaving the highway macadam, Sandy drove the truck while I followed, driving our tiny maroon Toyota sedan into the dirt road's shadowy cavern of towering trees. Malta's purrs seemed to echo Northwest Bay Brook. It burbled close by, contained within its banks; March's ugly face forgotten. We drove through pine groves so tall and thick they blocked out the sun. They had been planted in the 1930s by the Civilian Conservation Corps (CCC) to reclaim farm fields.

As we neared the tree-clogged cellar holes of the abandoned thousand-acre Alma Farm—right where the road had flooded in March—Sandy thrust his arm out, pointing to a white-tailed deer prancing across the road in front of the truck. Slowing for the bridge, we then turned right to pass the former Wardboro schoolhouse, now a hunting camp. Its owner, Sheriff Patrolman Kibby French, had called us in Massachusetts just the previous fall to warn us about break-ins in all the camps on the road. We felt indebted to him, but he wasn't there today to watch our caravan pass. Next door, Pete and Mary Gorrie's neat, white board camp also sat empty, although they often drove the thirty miles from their home to enjoy this retreat, particularly during deer hunting season. Pete had given us a hand building our back shed and porch.

Approaching where we had turned around in March, I whooped and followed the truck past the drop off. The tires grated on the gravelly road as we passed a series of cellar holes, now nearly invisible in overgrown fields and planted pines. Ahead on a hillside, I caught a glimpse of the green shingled home of Marc and Nora Merrill. Now in their eighties, they migrated to Florida in the winter and had not yet returned. They were like family. Tiny curly-haired Nora had been Sandy's first babysitter, and later, her husband Marc had been Sandy's first boss at the Grand Union. As a young child, Marc had lived down the road in his grandfather's farmhouse. He knew the landscape as both a deer hunter and a man with a great love for the Valley's human history.

He had told us about the first farmers, the Wards, who had left Chester, Vermont, in horse drawn wagons in 1806, looking for land. Not much is known about the trip that Sandy's ancestors, Zachariah and his brother Deacon John Ward, made as they set out with their wives and children. I imagined they had many days of hard travel before they reached the old Military Road that brought them south out of Ticonderoga into the valley drained by the network of upland streams that feed Northwest Bay Brook.

Perhaps the wagons lurched and horses stumbled coming over the steep track, along the now abandoned road that stretches downhill into Wardboro Valley and comes out just beyond our house. I wondered if they saw deer and bear, as we do, or trembled to hear the nightly screams of panthers that we have never known. It was hard to imagine the work they faced, clearing forests to create farms. Perhaps the brooks flooded then, too, adding to the obstacles they faced as they created a community.

By the time Marc and Nora built their four-room home in 1966, they were the only Wardboro residents, although Marc's good friend, Jim Ross, often visited his beloved cabin a few miles farther north. For several years the Merrills lived in Wardboro year-round, commuting the eleven miles back and forth to Bolton each workday. Their home became a sanctuary from their frantic lives running the supermarket in a tourist town. Here they reveled in mountain views and wild animal neighbors, connected to a network of family and friends by a CB radio. Propane took the place of the electrical power that had never reached Wardboro.

Once we passed the Merrill's place, I knew Journey's End was now just a mile away: up steep Dan's Hill, past the topsy-turvy Wardboro Cemetery, over School House Brook's culvert, and past the remains of a Boy Scout camp owned by the Barretts from Great Barrington. Approaching Jim Grey's one-room shack, I felt my body relax, knowing our trip was nearing its end. Jim, a retired state policeman and real estate agent, devoted himself to his place. It had been named Wolf Camp by the sportswriter who had built it and kept hunting dogs in the basement. Jim was another person who really kept track of what was going on along Wardboro Road. Adventurers of sorts, all of us put up with humble living conditions and the moody road to share this special place.

Malta could feel my excitement building, for she prowled the seats, also anxious to explore the world rolling by. I stroked her tail as it swished by my nose and slowed the car to both drive and look. To my left, beyond tumbled-down stone walls, old farm fields merged into forested hills whose rolling ridges delineated the western side of the Valley. Off to the right beyond a tangle of bushes and small trees, Spectacle Ponds Brook meandered through the low fields, here and there dammed into ponds by generations of beavers. And beyond, when I stretched my neck, I could see Catamount—the small mountain whose 2,000-foot-plus ridgeline loomed to the east.

Looking back to the road, I nearly rear-ended the truck. Sandy had stopped.

"What's up?" I yelled.

"Washout ahead," he warned. Then he slowly moved forward, and I watched the truck lurch across a rocky hole. I maneuvered the Toyota off the edge of the road to bypass the worst of the erosion, apparently caused by a blocked culvert.

At last! We migrants were at our clearing. Our journey had taken us from Wayland's several thousand homes, streets, and businesses to Wardboro Valley where we two would be the only year-round human residents.

The settlement of farms where families could find help just down the road had lasted about one hundred years. By 1920 the descendents of the original settlers had migrated to farms in Iowa or moved to Bolton Landing looking for easier lives. Ours was a reverse migration: from easy living to pioneering. We looked forward to problem-solving without electric or phone lines, using primitive plumbing, and harvesting enough firewood from our 160 acres to keep warm in winter. We would put in gardens and try living simply. Most of all, we hankered to observe the network of creatures and plants already in place at Journey's End without disturbing their lives any more than necessary.

We came to settle on the margin, at the edge of human activity. Living along an edge is a risky proposition, for "things on the margins…are often on the brink of becoming something else." The day we arrived we thought only of the unknown adventure that lay ahead, not realizing how we ourselves might change in the process or that we might alter the life we found here.

The only way to understand a language like this
is to immerse yourself in it,
give yourself over to it, suspend judgment,
keep your eyes and ears open until it starts to make sense.

Kathleen Dean Moore, *River Walking: Reflections on Moving Water*

This Simple Life

The screech of frogs has taken over the marsh. I listen, bemused: a foreigner who doesn't know the language.

Hidden among pine trees on the knoll we call "the island", I am surrounded by beaver canals connecting a string of beaver ponds. No matter how hard I look along their edges, I find no frogs. I cock my left ear to identify exactly where each screamer is perched, but my deaf right ear makes sorting out their locations impossible. These spring peepers are so tiny and well camouflaged, I doubt I will ever find them. So I simply sit back, closing my eyes to absorb this May evening's sounds. Blue jay alarms suddenly pierce the froggy medley. Closer at hand I detect the scritch of a beaver snacking on twigs. Crickets twanging in the background are interrupted by more raucous cries of blue jays and more beaver munching.

When I open my eyes, at first I see nothing but Catamount Mountain. The sun has already set, but its reflected light makes the mountain appear to glow with its own ruddy brightness. Then I notice ripples in the pond that hint of feeding beavers. Slight "schlips" in the water tell tales of fish jumping, or maybe a frog leaping. Suddenly, a high-pitched, distant cry startles me, followed by more yowls and yips as several coyotes sound off somewhere to the south. For a few minutes their singing swells, showering me with sounds that I drink in, thirsty for this potion of wild music.

Listening and watching for animal stories had preoccupied us, even before we arrived that April day. During the summers that we helped Kitty and Ed, we often slept in a canvas tent pitched on the island, under the tall pines. We spied on beavers until dark forced us to just listen and guess what they were doing. Adding branches to a dam? Working on a house? Gnawing down a tree?

Later, when Sandy and I stretched out on our foam pad, my ears seemed to grow, as I listened to the tiny noises of unknowns moving around outside the tent. Then a blast of snorts sounded close by and we both sat up, completely awake. We clutched each other awaiting some sort of attack. When nothing happened, we lay down and, after awhile, slept uneasily. The next day, Kitty guessed that alarmed white-tailed deer had been scared into spreading word of our smelly presence.

The Valley has enveloped us with sights and sounds that keep our senses simmering. I want to immerse myself in the moment at hand; to empty myself and open up to receive other lives. We have a lot to learn to be able to decipher the goings-on of our wild companions. We want to copy the stealth of hunters, armed only with eyes and ears. To do that we need to hang out in the woods, trying to learn the skills of a deer or coyote. Or cat.

When Malta joins me on my way to the island, I try to imitate her slow stalk. Her entire being focuses on silently watching, smelling, listening, feeling her surroundings. I step carefully and think I am paying attention, but I can't match her talent for observing wildlife. While I have become alarmed at her killing habits, which have already ended the lives of chickadees, mice, and moles, I admire her hunting prowess. I find myself constantly astir. Too easily my thoughts bounce from Malta to yesterday's argument, then to tomorrow's hiking plans. She has the patience to settle into a place and endlessly await action. I want to do that too.

I also want to wander the road and old logging trails, getting acquainted with the emerging wildflowers. Even though I know the flowers don't care about charming me, I am charmed. And impressed—with how these plants advertise themselves to pollinators. Their message is loud and clear, even to me. Come fertilize me and I'll feed you. Both the flowers and the attracted insects or birds benefit, exchanging dining for sexual services.

I fumble with my newly purchased second-hand non-automatic camera, carefully taking their portraits before the blooms pass by. It seems I am following a parade. It is led by early purple or white hepaticas and dainty pink-striped spring beauties. A week later maroon three-petaled trillium edge the road, white-flagged Dutchmen's breeches carpet a hillside, and nodding gold trout lily bells decorate a drainage ditch.

While I am tempted to pick the trout lilies' blossoms, I notice that their patches of pointed gray-green leaves have few flowers. When I read, later, that only the few two-leaved plants will flower and only after several years, I am glad I only took their pictures. Returning a few weeks later, I search for the leaves and flowers in vain, for they have dropped off, enriching the earth from which they grew.

Sandy's focus on firewood sends him on tree identification forays. He pores over tree guidebooks trying to decide which trees are which in our woods. Jim Grey, Marc Merrill, and Frank Dagles (an experienced woodsman from town) happily advise him about the best firewood trees.

"Ash—that's what you want," insists Frank. "You can cut ash while it's green and get good heat out of it." Once Sandy starts looking, he discovers many tall, straight white ash trees that cut like butter. He gets busy with his chain saw, knowing these logs may help us stay warm this first year, when little time is left to collect a wood supply. At first the forest seemed like a treasure to be preserved. Not wanting to topple any trees, he cut mostly those that had already fallen. Now he realizes that thinning trees can lead to a healthier woodlot. He studies each tree to learn who it is, considers its age and diameter and whether its neighborhood is too crowded.

Wandering our acres, he lusts after the leaf shapes of beech, oak, yellow birch, cherry, and sugar maple. He slicks his hand over the smooth gray bark of American beech trees and the rough, horizontally-banded bark of yellow birch. He finds hop hornbeam with its muscular wood, and then struggles to split it. Once he cuts the birch, red oak, or cherry their fruity aroma tantalizes us. The cherry's reddish hue makes it almost too special to burn. I mark sugar maples with red plastic strips so we will know who they are mid-winter when we want to tap them to make syrup.

Our heating system includes an ancient wood cookstove that dominates the kitchen and the All-Nighter that stands close to the fireplace in the living room. Whether they will keep us warm this winter depends on our keeping them stoked with wood. Sandy's eyes shine and sweat dribbles down his neck, as he lunges with the axe to split hunk after hunk. Now and then he stops to ogle the mountain, or listen to a male grouse drumming on a log. I try my hand too, always startled when the axe actually hits the wood and two pieces fly off.

One day the axe comes close to my foot, and I pause to wonder, "What are we going to do if we have an emergency? What if one of the kids has an emergency? How will they let us know?" Our three children, now adults, live in Rhode Island, Pennsylvania, and Oregon, and we regret how hard it is to keep in touch with them. While we like the idea of living beyond power lines, I begin to wonder if we will be happy living without a phone.

When I explain our situation to Jay at a cell phone company, he jumps at the challenge, agreeing to bring his cell phone and try it out. We meet him in town and lead the way back, along Lake George. Then we bump along the dirt road, under all those trees. Once we arrive at our homesite, he steps from his car, scratching his head.

"You won't believe it, but the phone had service only twice on this road, including right here!" Over Sandy's lasagna lunch, we talk possibilities. They are limited by the interfering mountains and forests. We decide to chance it, and install a cell phone in the truck. Then the fun begins. Sometimes we have to drive around to find a spot where the phone will work. After we turn it on for an hour in the evening, incoming calls honk the truck's horn and one of us rushes out, hoping to catch the caller. We soon discover that this fragile tie to the rest of the world creates just one more project to keep us busy and adds a layer of frustration to our lives when it doesn't work.

Now we sleep in the house on a futon tucked into the living room. When I arise I find plenty of distractions to interfere with beaver pond spying and flower study. I can weed the perennial flower garden, spade the vegetable patch, write in my journal, make bread, shake rugs, or sweep the always dusty floor. I can try my hand at splitting firewood. All these to do…and more. I look around trying to decide what to do first, and find it hard to believe that this simple life can present so many decisions to puzzle over.

For Malta, there is no problem—she just plunges into Wardboro life, prowling her new territory at all hours, scarcely taking time for a catnap. At the same time I spin erratically through the turmoil of daily tasks. Plodding outside to water the peppers, I notice the hummingbird feeder needs refilling. Setting down the watering can, I fetch the feeder inside, heat water on the stove, wash the glass tube and fill it with crystal clear sugar syrup. When I stretch to rehang the feeder above the foxgloves, I recall wanting to dry some of the fragrant bunches of white yarrow that grow nearby. After snipping the stems and hanging them high in the dim rafters of the airy shed, I realize the floor below needs to be swept. Once that is done, it's time to stop for soup and bread. Then, I remember—I never watered the peppers.

I pause to wonder why I ever thought living closer to nature would lead to simplicity, for there is so much more we need to do for ourselves in Wardboro. We both struggle to prioritize what's important, because everywhere we look, tasks await. Maybe the secret is that we need to slow down and become human *be-ings*, content to live moment by moment.

Is it the need to do that complicates life? Sandy, the take-action man, seems most happy when he moves from task to task, knowing what he will do next. On the other hand, I prefer to plunge through the day. When I weed, I put my all into it. I notice the texture of the stem, its leaves, the darkness of the soil, the beetle or worm I unearth, the fragrance of the nearby basil, the blue sky overhead, the black flies crawling on my neck.

Each day also offers us opportunities for camaraderie that were impossible in Wayland where, too often, our lives separated into two strands that did not intertwine easily. Learning to focus our lives in Wardboro gives us new appreciation of each other that we gain when we rub shoulders tackling chores unknown in our past lives. When we share the fields, woods, and streams we find we both delight in the hidden lives that emerge.

As our language grows—and we can name that red oak or these bracken ferns or those purple-flowered raspberry plants or this golden Alexander flower or that yellow birch—the Valley sprouts with acquaintances with whom we feel comfortable.

In June I investigate a congregation of large yellow blooms happy in water up to their ankles. My new Newcomb's Wildflower Guidebook tells me they are *caltha palustris*—marsh marigold or cowslip. Leaves and stems may be cooked as a green. I kneel as close as I can without getting wet, and take a photo of them with a new close-up lens. Wanting to save a few of the five-petaled flowers and their umbrella-shaped leaves before their brief lives pass, I stop worrying about dry feet and pick several, careful to avoid pulling up their roots. I want to preserve this beautiful community, so I will not harvest these bright beings for greens. Back at the house I slip the petals into protective tissue and press them between boards. Next winter the pressed flowers will remind me of the treasures awaiting, once the year turns.

Tending to the house and its five cleared acres works long-unused muscles and forces us to try out new problem-solving skills. Sandy, who used to work on public health issues, now enthusiastically splits wood or installs plumbing. I, who enjoyed sorting out human problems, struggle when it comes to figuring out what makes things work. I love the hours immersed in the gardens, digging up seed beds, or carrying off a crop of rocks before the seeds and seedlings can be planted in the dark soil. By nightfall we collapse into bed. All around us, projects pressure us to keep working.

Water is a worry. Dean Phillips (who built Journey's End in 1860) had hauled it from a spring a couple hundred feet down the road. Uphill, in the woods behind the house, the spring Kitty and Ed found bubbles out of bedrock filling an upended culvert used as a storage tank. An above-ground plastic pipe carries this precious cargo to the house. We hope this simple system will give us water for drinking, cooking, hand-washing dishes, and bathing. Maybe there is enough pressure for occasionally wetting down gardens, but not for toilet flushing. On July days when our water pressure dwindles, we poke around the well with shovels, anxiously looking for leaks.

There is no lack of invigorating, icy water in Spectacle Pond Brook, 150 yards from the house. As July turns sizzling, we wander uphill along the unmaintained road, passing through a cool tunnel of maples, beeches, oaks, and birches. After rustling through tall ferns we descend the wooded ridge to the brook. We stand at the base of a vertical rock wall, dwarfed by a thirty-foot waterfall that cascades into a shallow pool at our feet.

Off come the clothes and Sandy is already reclining in the shivery pool, while I inch my way in. The change in temperature is shocking, but the pool is so inviting with its flat rock seats that allow me to gradually immerse myself. I join water striders who are scurrying across the water's surface and settle into the chill. My relaxation ends abruptly when I sense somebody nibbling my toes. Jumping with alarm, I giggle at the school of tiny fish who flash away. As we refrigerate, we wonder about the cavern that is forming next to the falls, where large chunks of rock reveal the power of water as it seeps, freezes, and thaws. We are weaklings when it comes to managing water.

Back at the house, we face a waste water disposal problem. The only plumbing we have leads from the kitchen sink into a rocky pit behind the house. The pipe drains poorly, and liquid sometimes leaches into the basement through the old field-stone walls. Each time he watches water back-up in the sink, Sandy ponders the problem. By August he has an idea. He will start at the well, following the pipe downhill where it lies atop the seasonal streamlet we call Kitty's Creek. With coffee cup in hand, he pulls me outside, where he explains what he wants to do.

"I'm going to sink the pipe as it crosses the yard toward the house—maybe three feet deep by the creek and ten feet close to the basement. Then I'll bring the water pipe into the house under the south cellar wall," he points his cup. "The drainage pipe can go back out through the same hole and feed into a pit I'll dig fifteen feet from the house where the yard slopes away."

My mouth opens and closes silently, and I almost drop my cup of tea. "Bring the pipes under the basement wall?" I finally say, "You're kidding."

"We'll just do it a little at a time, and before we know it we'll have a plumbing system," he enthuses, his blue eyes bright with excitement.

The next day, with sweat dripping, he shovels in the side yard until he disappears from view. When I try to dig alongside, we just get in each other's way, rather like what happens in the kitchen. At Journey's End I am no longer chief cook, for Sandy has become a flamboyant chef, eager to make meals too. To forestall bickering, we each do our own thing in the kitchen—on different days.

In the trench, my five and one-half foot frame is also not up to the job. Once the trench is six feet deep, when I manage to thrust a shovelful of dirt over my head, the debris lands back at my feet. Not much help. So I become the rock toter. As Sandy heaves rocks and stones of all sizes and shapes, I lug them to a separate pile that mounds as his trench deepens.

Days later, his spirits flag, for it seems he will never reach the bottom of the field-stone basement wall. And then his shovel breaks through, and his aching tiredness evaporates. After taking a breather he turns to excavate a pit away from the house and discovers enormous boulders blocking his way.

"Oh well, who said this was going to be easy?" he grunts as he attacks the barriers with shovel and crowbar.

Next comes the nitty-gritty work of installing the black plastic pipe. First he must drill through kitchen floorboards and basement ceiling boards to make a hole for the kitchen sink pipe. There are heavy beams and basement stone walls to avoid. There is no electricity to ease the work! Sandy patiently drills a hole, but before he gets very far, the hand drill breaks. Grumbling, he replaces the bit only to have it shortly break again.

"I was really ready for a break," he grins, rubbing his cramped arm while I wipe the grime off his face.

"How can you be so patient?" I ask, admiring his persistence. "I would be screaming or crying about now."

"Well, it's just something I really want to do," he replies. "And I know if I keep at it, I will get the job done—somehow."

I puzzle over why I am so impatient with anything that really challenges my problem-solving skills. My father was an engineer who delighted in solving problems and I was convinced he could figure out how to do anything. While my older sister Ellen and I helped when he built a barn for my mother's horses and a family tennis court on our rural ten acres in Delaware, we simply followed his directions. I never understood how he did the figuring. Furthermore, as a teenager, I didn't want to be like him. I preferred to escape such projects by riding horseback across our fields to the miles of adjacent farm and forest lands. To his disappointment, I became an adult with little self-confidence when it came to practical hands-on projects.

Even so, I oversaw our home front after Sandy and I married, for he was preoccupied: first, with his medical studies, and later with the demands of internship, residency, and physician-hood. I solved the problems as best I could, pulling him in to decipher malfunctioning toilets, leaking faucets, and childhood illnesses. Coming to Journey's End has opened up a whole new world for him, and he has emerged as a fanatic do-it-yourselfer. I have adjusted by taking on my mother's role as advisor and follower, pleased to have a leader. I watch him as he finally enlarges the hole with a new bit and then carefully expands it with his handsaw. Maybe some of his patience will rub off on me, and I can try to avoid my knee-jerk reactions of frustration. Many minutes later his saw reaches the basement air and we celebrate over a soup lunch.

Getting both the water and drainage pipes inserted into the trench, and under the basement wall, makes us wish for the arms of an octopus. Once we pull those long black snakes into the basement, the real work begins as we try to avoid the twelve sawed-off trees that support the house beams. To do this we dance in the dark, balancing a flashlight while urging the pipe along. The semi-rigid pipe seems to have a mind of its own, shifting uneasily every time Sandy starts to make a connection. He groans and cusses as he tussles with it, until the system settles into place. A dousing with boiling water finally solidifies the connections, including the shunt to the hoped-for tub.

Bathing is a quandary. While satisfied with cold water from the faucet that we heat in large pots on either the wood cookstove or the tiny propane stove, I am not happy relying on sponge baths. The metal washtub we brought was a big disappointment. After Sandy helped fill it, I climbed in and cautiously settled down in the warm brew. I splashed, soaped, washed, and sort-of rinsed but couldn't figure out how to give myself a shampoo. When we struggled to drain off the water, it took both of us to push the washtub across the floor with water sloshing before we could empty it off the front porch. While I can see why Wardboro farmers did not take many baths, I'm not sure I want to live year in and year out like this.

Standing at the kitchen window I realize the birds have figured out how to turn the nearby streamlet into a bathing spa. A junco shakes itself vigorously in a small pool, splashing water to clean its feathers, again and again. Later I watch the frenzied antics of several finches and a robin who agitate the water to moisten themselves. For the summer, we move our bathing outside too, to an outdoor sun-shower hanging in an out-of-the-way spot on the back wall of the shed. After heating in the sun all day, the black plastic bag dribbles its treasure of liquid warmth as I stand washing body and hair in the company of ruby-throated hummingbirds who buzz back and forth to a nearby feeder. While this has to be the ultimate in bathing, I dream of a real tub for winter, connected to both cold water and a drainage pipe. We puzzle almost daily over where to find one, and where to put such a thing in this bathroom-less house.

On a trip to town, I bump into Theta Curri, one of Kitty's elementary school friends. She looks at me strangely when I bemoan our lack of tub.

"You know, I have just what you need. I'm selling a small claw-footed tub that belonged to the last Wardboro school teacher who recently died." I stare with disbelief. Well, of course, the tub must come here! We puzzle over where to put it; finally settling on the southeastern corner of the kitchen, close to the cookstove.

Sandy transports the tiny tub in the truck and deposits it on the front porch, where we circle it admiringly. Since it needs a little brightening, it sits there for a few days while I scrape and sand its bottom and paint it white. With the claw feet reattached, the tub emerges as a personality, calling out for a place of its own. That same day we haul it to its corner, and Sandy spends an afternoon drilling and sawing to install the cold water and drain pipes, and connect the fittings to the tub. It now feels like a new member of the family. With trepidation he turns on the faucet. We watch with shocked grins as the cold water flows into the tub without a single leak.

Then we test this marvel. I heat two large pots of water and pour them in, adding just enough cold water from the faucet to produce an inviting concoction. Even though I must sit with my knees almost up to my chest in order to fit, it feels like a fancy hot tub. With the sun shower added to a hook in the ceiling, I can soak in the tub, while also getting a shampoo. When I pull the plug, the tub empties; just like that!

Knowing that winter is coming keeps us puttering our way through the summer, one day at a time. Still we take time to play, adventuring to the other side of Lake George to climb Black Mountain and enjoy its panoramic views. One day we hike the old road out of the Valley and find beaver wetlands and a beautiful isolated pond. We also follow Spectacle Pond Brook and Flybrook, using them as paths into the landscape, confident we will not get lost. When we struggle up Dean's Hill (behind the house) looking for its top, the summit eludes us. The way back is easy to find; all downhill to the road. I marvel at how we both love these rambles. We seem to catch each other's excitement over unfamiliar flowers, ambling salamanders, beaver gnawings, and squirrel stashes.

Exploring the traces of an old farm road taken over by trees is more of a challenge. I get so turned around hunting for its route that when we arrive at a pine-filled bluff, I feel completely lost.

"Where are we?" I ask in a fear-choked voice that I don't recognize as mine. I stare at a stream trickling below and a wooded hill beyond. Everything looks unfamiliar. Sandy looks around and then stares at me quizzically.

"There's Flybrook below and the road is just uphill a bit. We are almost home."

Unbelieving, I stare back at him. Then with a twist of my head, I look again, and my fear leaves. Reality floods my eyes. The landscape shifts, and becomes familiar. Of course, I know where we are!

The only challenge now is to get across the stream. The route of the old road is very clear as we follow where it was cut out of the steep hillside. Beyond, we teeter across a tree trunk that fell completely across the stream. Journey's End is an easy stroll past the Wardboro Cemetery.

As summer dwindles, I consider the outhouse. This handsome rebuilt two-seater adds character to the backyard; its surrounding flowers inviting me to visit. I also use it as a blind, and sit with the door open, watching. Often gray squirrels entertain me. They chatter from pine-tops where they industriously toss cones into piles for later dining. Before cold weather makes the outhouse unfriendly to use, we want to create an indoor waterless composting toilet system. Almost every eleven-mile mail trip to town brings how-to literature that we peruse in the evenings, trying to picture what will work here. I fall asleep at night puzzling.

The house itself is a puzzle. We are thankful for the propane tanks that allow a small gas cookstove, a 1950s refrigerator-freezer (rescued from a Marlboro, Massachusetts kitchen renovation project), and seven downstairs propane lights. Upstairs we use flashlights or camping battery lamps. We have no electric lights since no power lines are strung into the Valley. The only appliance I miss is the vacuum cleaner. Sweeping or mopping the old wooden floors just rearranges all the dust, garden soil, cat hair, and other dirt we leave behind.

Sandy locates a small second-hand generator for sale at his friend Freddy Brickner's mechanic business in town and lugs it home in the back of the truck. With just a quick pull of the starting cord he easily gets it grumbling, while I often struggle unsuccessfully. Once it roars to life, it rumbles from its perch in the back shed, and allows us to use our vacuum cleaner again. Somehow, being able to really clean up and make our mark, if just on the house's innards, is important to do.

Not that everything inside is under control. We need to do something about the badly deteriorating plaster walls that line the narrow steep stairway going to the second floor, where two tiny rooms are crammed along the southern wall. I hate to touch the old walls upstairs as they shower plaster at the least excuse and dribble hunks of disintegrating wallpaper. A large unfinished room stretches across the northern half, where bats still infiltrate. While we must tackle the upstairs renovation and add insulation to use less wood in the winter, this will have to wait. There is so much else we simply must do first. For the time being, we avoid the second floor.

It is becoming clear that simple living in the Wardboro Valley is not so simple after all. All the distracting needs push and pull us. Some days they are overwhelming. Most of the time, we try to shrug off our worries. We work our way slowly through the obstacles, but also let our senses overload on mountains, woods, rushing streams, bird song, and summer's tranquil times. We slip off to get better acquainted, especially with the island.

Journal entry: September 10

On this September evening the light dims. Bats take to the airways above the pond. Silently they swoop, high, then low, looking for insects. Their erratic acrobatics leave me wondering if one might come nibble mosquitoes on my ear, except I've not heard any mosquito whines tonight. The bats never approach me. I am of no interest to them as they flit their wordless predatory dance in the ever more shadowy evening.

Then the ducks come, diving out of the sky, announcing themselves with mini-jet airplane noises when they put on their brakes to splash down to a sudden halt in the pond. At first I can see them through binoculars: black ducks, mallards, a frowsy female wood duck and her handsome consorts. Soon they become invisible in the dark. Mallard quacks and male wood duck peeps punctuate the night while the female wood duck's come hither wail, "ook...a...le-e-e," pierces my brain. Wing flaps splatter water expressing avian disagreements.

Stealing away, I marvel at the lives I have witnessed at the pond. Although I don't understand much about them, it seems my relationship to them is shifting. After these hours of watching and listening, I feel more connected to wood ducks, coyotes, frogs, bats and beavers. I am no longer completely separate, a stranger isolated outside the network of Valley beings. I belong here, too. I am beginning to understand the lingo.

Home: A place where one likes to be;

A restful, congenial place...

The place that is the natural environment of an animal, plant...

Webster's New World College Dictionary

Homesteading

Sandy creaks open the screen door to let Malta out for her nightly hunt. Overhead a nearly full moon shines so brightly that the house casts a shadow across the yard. I am missing from the picture, for I need to spend the week in Massachusetts finishing work at the Senior Center. As the cat disappears into the dark yard, Sandy immerses himself in moonlight before returning to the book he's reading about the Revolutionary War. While he loves to forage on such volumes now that he doesn't always have to have his nose in a medical book or journal, he decides it's too dark to continue reading. Besides, he doesn't want to light the noisy propane lamp. Drawn to the living room futon, he falls asleep listening to barred owl hoots.

He awakes to a noise. Something vibrating…somewhere. A peculiar scritching—very persistent—maybe just outside. Yawning, he checks his watch…2:30 A.M. He stumbles to the screen door, the noise stops, and Malta slips inside.

"What you been up to?" The cat flips her tail and rubs his legs, just as the sound erupts again. He fumbles for a flashlight, steps onto the front porch and flashes his beam around. There…gnawing on one of the porch supports. A large bristly porcupine!

"Hey, get away!" When the creature pays him no mind and continues chewing, Sandy picks up a shovel and tries to shove the animal away from the house. But Porky isn't leaving. He just keeps munching.

"Grunt…grunt…grunt," is his only response. Sandy's blood pressure skyrockets. He lets loose a couple of solid blows, and the porcupine crumples into a prickly heap. Motionless! He pokes the animal inquiringly.

"My God! I've killed him," he groans. Dazed, he picks the corpse up by one paw and wheelbarrows the invader into the woods. Then, wide awake, he flops back onto the futon and tosses and turns the night away trying to figure out if somehow he could have deterred the relentless beast without killing it. "Whose house is this anyhow?" his tired brain keeps asking.

I return to find Sandy feeling like a murderer. We had hoped to live peaceably in this seemingly quiet place—watching wildlife, not violently ending their lives.

"Carl used to tell me about how porcupines terrorized Journey's End years ago," Sandy remembers. "They went crazy over wood, but especially plywood, and anything salty. Outhouses really attracted them, lured by the smell of humans."

I point to the patched hole in the living room wall. "One did some serious chewing there at one time. Are we going to have to fight the porkies for the house?"

"I doubt it. Fishers have become much more common, and they are champions at flipping porcupines and feeding on them—belly first." According to Marc these dog-sized mammals with long bushy tails are all around us; good creatures to have on our side as we try to make this house a home.

Journey's End has a way of upending our expectations. Even commonplace objects like a kitchen appliance can lead to adventure. The large, old propane refrigerator-freezer that we bought for $100 back in Massachusetts is like a prima donna who demands solicitous attention. On the one hand, I feel lucky to have an appliance with both refrigeration and freezing capability. On the other hand, her dependability is questionable. On a hot, humid summer day she goes on strike, which brings Sandy to her side. Following the refrigerator manual's advice he hits the thermostat cautiously with a hammer to try to dislodge any dirt. The temperature still hovers above fifty degrees.

The phone allows us to call the local propane serviceman, who comes to visit. He doesn't seem to know as much about the refrigerator as Sandy. One look at the elderly appliance and the man cautions, "You know you have to watch out for these old Servels. They can give off deadly carbon monoxide gas—they aren't legal to sell any more."

Just as we are ready to give up and pay big bucks for a new propane refrigerator, we remember Ozzie, a Servel master mechanic who lives in Barton, Vermont. Sandy tracks him down. Again the phone comes through for us, and Ozzie tries to diagnose, long-distance, the refrigerator's condition.

"You better buy a carbon monoxide alarm and put it up in the kitchen," he says first thing. "You'll be safe enough. Just clean out her burning chamber and exhaust from time to time." He finally opines, "Ya know, what she probably needs is burping. That ammonia gas those babies use can jell, and then you can't do nothing with them. You'll just have to turn her upside down."

After looking at the cantankerous machine for a few days, we decide to carry out the prescription. It takes both of us. I haul all the food onto the kitchen counter. Sandy carefully disconnects the pipes from the gas, and we shove the old girl unwillingly to center kitchen. We stare at the six-foot fat lady, trying to figure how we will ever get her topsy-turvy. Sliding a low bench close to her front, Sandy tips the refrigerator and then pulls her toward him. I push from the back. Pull…Push…Push… She inches unwillingly onto the bench. Then, suddenly, she slides, while we hang on to ease her passage, from right-side up to upside-down. Breathing hard, I gawk with disbelief at the refrigerator standing on her head. I sure hope the ammonia is circulating.

A few days later when we team up again to turn her over, we find she still is hardly functioning. We no sooner decide we will have to go with a new refrigerator, when the weather cools.

The lady reluctantly goes back to work. We decide to stick by her as we now know her innards better than any refrigerator we've ever owned. But we pay attention to that carbon monoxide alarm.

During fall's cooler days we shift our cooking from the tiny propane stove to its neighbor, the gargantuan black wood cookstove. It also serves as our furnace. In Wayland I would flip a switch to light the electric stove or simply pop open the microwave. Here I must first light a fire. I poke crunched up newspaper, kindling, and wood into the fire-box. After opening the air vents, I light a match and stand back. Without enough air the wood smolders; its acrid smoke rushes out the stove's cracks while I cough and choke, fiddle with vents, yell for Sandy, and rush to open all the doors. If the fire catches, the stove top becomes hot with possibilities. I can boil water closest to the fire, and simmer soup at the right-hand edge.

The oven keeps me guessing. Its temperature gauge only approximates the interior heat, and changes depending on the burning going on in the firebox. When I spend the morning making bread, I usually bake in the propane oven, unwilling to experiment with the woodstove. Too often it either burns the loaves or leaves their centers uncooked. Sandy is the risk-taker who will trust his bread, muffins, or casserole to the wood stove.

This first December disappoints us when it brings not snow but rain to welcome our first guests: our daughter Bonnie, her husband Murray, and their two dogs. They no sooner arrive from Rhode Island for a pre-Christmas get-together than the downpours start. After three days, Malta and the dogs explode outside, and we follow. North of the house, the seasonal stream has fled its banks to wash over the road. Thankful for mist instead of pattering rain, we stretch our legs and listen to the crescendo of water. Strolling to the bridge high above Spectacle Pond Brook, we watch the flow churn by.

All this water in such a hurry leaves me overwhelmed and speculative. As the uplands shed the rain, I imagine it seeping from the overflow of hillside springs, trickling through crevices, eroding soil to create rocky streamlets. They drain into larger brooks that wash into Spectacle Pond Brook and Fly Brook before merging with Northwest Bay Brook and finally flowing into Lake George.

Deciding not to let the weather affect us, we join Murray in his van to drive to a movie in Glens Falls. When we get a view of Fly Brook curling close to the bottom of the high embankment, we stare, impressed. It has risen several feet. The van becomes quiet as the power of the brook silences our tongues. Nobody says it, but we all wonder, "Will the road be flooded?" A couple of minutes later, we know the answer, for the broad bridge that usually dominates the scraggly brook barely contains the thrusting flood pouring out of the Valley.

Murray drives on anyway. Around the first curve the road disappears—only water as far as we can see. Suddenly the movie has no appeal.

"Poker!" demands Bonnie. "You promised a good poker game like we used to play with Helen. Now's the time."

The brook roars defiantly as we motor deliberately back to Journey's End. This time we are flooded inside the Valley. We sit tight, enjoying the watershed in action.

The weeks after the flood usher in below-freezing weather. Each day brings something new to figure out. Although Sandy delights in using his muscles and mind to smooth out the rough edges of our new lifestyle, I wonder, as the days grow colder, how we are going to manage. Learning to feed the stoves to keep us comfortable, yet not waste wood is crucial. Although I am impressed by the piles of wood stacked outside and in the shed, Sandy predicts that before spring arrives, all will be gone. He keeps the elephantine kitchen stove stuffed and shakes his head over its greedy habits compared with the efficient little air-tight stove connected to the living room's chimney. The old house leaks the heat they produce like a sieve.

We treat the propane tanks with respect, for they allow us refrigeration, a back-up cookstove, and downstairs lights. As the dark evenings lengthen, I dance with a long-handled butane lighter, learning how to ignite each wall lamp's cloth mantle without destroying its flimsy material by getting too close. We use these frugally, always considering whether a lamp is really needed and turning it off when we leave a room. "How's the tank?" becomes our mantra. We certainly don't want to run out of propane.

With winter's arrival, perhaps the only thing automatic about Journey's End is the cold water that flows so clear and icy from our two indoor faucets. To keep it from freezing, Sandy has rigged the pipe so that it also sprays outdoors at the end of the above-ground waterline, creating a froth of ice. Day after day the temperature dips below zero. One morning when I roll out of the futon, I gasp as my feet touch the cold floor and shiver back under the covers. Sandy calls from the kitchen, "It was -20° last night," and turns on the faucet to brush his teeth. All he gets is a blast of cold air. Our waterline has frozen.

December's deluge seems like a pipe dream. Before the morning is over, we begin hauling that precious fluid from the enclosed road spring that hasn't frozen. When I hike the 150 feet down the road to the spring, I carry two plastic gallon jugs at a time while Sandy manages four. Within a few days, walking for water becomes just part of what we do every day. These trips offer opportunities to look for tracks of deer or coyotes passing by, to listen to the creaks and cracks of the winter woods, and to check for birds, mice, or squirrels attracted to our feeders. I set the jug under the spigot and absorb the quiet road with its stark edge trees. Then the second jug fills while I watch the tops of giant pine trees sway in the chill wind. As I walk back, I may be welcomed by blue jay alarms or chickadee greetings.

One snowy day I haul four gallons in the morning and four in the afternoon while Sandy brings back eleven. This is more than we need but we don't want to stagger back and forth during the storm that is forecast for the next day. Carrying in our water supply makes us very observant of how much we use. We guess it takes four or five gallons for each bath in the tub. I soon empathize with the Wardboro farmers who walked to the spring year in and year out to bring back their water. Unlike them, we get a reprieve in March.

On a melting morning Sandy awakes at 5:30 to the sound of gushing water. At first he thinks it is raining hard. Getting up in a sleepy fog, he finally realizes water is pouring out of the pipeline he opened in the basement when the freeze-up happened. He awakes in a hurry to vault down the dark, hazardous basement steps and stop the flood. The spray pipe outdoors won't thaw until spring's warmth finally settles in.

Our winter without running water makes old Wardboro feel very real. Marc and Nora Merrill have served as guides, for they have scouted cellar holes, forded Fly Brook to follow traces of a racetrack across a wooded plateau, and talked with folks who remembered the old days. Marc enthralls us with these stories and a collection of fading photos of earlier folks and their homes.

Ninety-one-year-old Madaline Ross remembers living in our house about 1918 when she was a small girl. She shivers recalling how cold it was when she and her sister slept in the unheated upstairs. Wardboro families farmed among rocks and stumps in the summer. In the winter the men spent long cold days in the mountains, logging. While some trees were cut for lumber, hemlock bark was hauled by horse and sled to a tannery miles away in Horicon. The families lived very self-sufficient lives in a world of hard labor, dirt, and insects (with no screened windows). The pungent smells from animal and human wastes that collected in barns and outhouses would have chased us away.

The house is littered with remnants of those early farming years. In the upstairs room where the bats infiltrate, we found glass kerosene lamps, crosscut saws, ice tongs, and the tines of a pitch fork. Newsprint plastered to one wall advertised a stud horse for hire at the Alma Farm two miles away where the road floods. Digging in gardens we have unearthed pottery chips and part of a china doll. An old hay rake lies under pine needles on the island and a plow seat poses in the woods on the high flat plateau down the road. Apple trees, lilacs, and daylilies still bloom each spring by cellar holes, echoing those newly replanted at Journey's End.

These folks had something special that we don't have: a year-round human community. By 1858 there were twenty-three houses, two schools, and four sawmills along Fly Brook. Though many families had left by the turn of the century, there were still neighbors to turn to for help. Willie and Cora Norton did that the year their baby Earl got so sick with fever that he lay limp in Cora's lap. Willie rushed him through the woods, along the road to get help from another family. But, like so much else of life then, there was nothing anyone could do, and the baby died. At least the neighbors could help shoulder the sadness.

Striving to get acquainted with the former Wardboro residents has taken us to the dappled shade of the community cemetery where tombstones lean haphazardly, their etched surfaces disappearing under a gauze of spreading lichen. Of the thirty people buried here, many were children who died during the Civil War years. Since there are no death records to turn to, we have wondered whether returning soldiers brought home typhoid. It must have felt as if death was stalking the Valley, perhaps also leading to the departure of more settlers. When we wander the cemetery, pondering the names and trying to picture these people, the graves help bring old Wardboro back to life.

Those old-time Wardboro farmers would not have understood our preoccupation with indoor running water, nor the work we are willing to undertake to get it. We have become convinced that we must sink the waterline. Sandy starts to dig the four-hundred-foot trench connecting house to well, planning to make it four feet deep to insure the pipe won't freeze. He gets nowhere quickly. Since his shovel keeps striking immovable rock, we hire a contractor who brings his backhoe one October day to dig that trench. The enormous boulders he excavates decorate the edge of the backyard, reminders of the enormity of our earthly underpinnings and our insignificance here.

Before we can lay any pipe, Sandy notices his thyroid gland has become swollen. Worried, we travel back to Massachusetts for a medical opinion since we don't have a local doctor yet. Results of an ultrasound report cancer. Cancer! I refuse to believe it. I stroke his neck, feeling the swelling, and hug his trim body that Journey's End has tested and found worthy. No, it can't be! Sandy, accepting the cancer diagnosis better than I, visits a surgeon. This doctor quickly determines that lab reports have gotten mixed up! There is no cancer. However, Sandy does need an operation to remove part of the thyroid, and it is scheduled.

During our two-week stay in Massachusetts, the southern Adirondacks are swept with days of rain that flood the ditch. When we return, with Sandy an impatient convalescent, we find water has also moved sideways from the trench, into the basement. It is hard to be upbeat about the situation, but we are so thankful to be back with Sandy's health returned to him, that we just try to work on tiny pieces of this mess. With Sandy supervising and attempting to stay on the sidelines, we finally drain off most of the water. Unfortunately, the flooding has left behind lots of soil. This means the trench is no longer deep enough to keep the pipe from freezing.

Trench duty is an amazingly awful experience. The loose, soupy soil grabs at my rubber boots and I truly get stuck in the mud. I then work to shovel the muck out of the watery mix and lift the heavy load onto shoulder-high dirt piles while my feet remain immovable. Sandy watches my inept struggles for a few hours before he too jumps in. We are both given a reprieve when Bonnie and Murray come to help and get caught up in the mire. They slog uphill across the yard into the woods toward the well. As soon as we can measure a depth of forty-four inches, we compromise on our goal of four feet and they sink the pipe. Then we celebrate. A month later I watch the backhoe fill in the trench, and cross my fingers that this underground piping will work all year.

I ponder how important water is to us, and realize that it is at least as critical to the beavers across the road in the marsh. Their ancestors probably arrived just after the last farmers left around 1920. Over the years, the beavers changed the old hay fields into a series of small beaver ponds with interlacing canals and pools. Their residences and dams change, almost yearly, as they move about seeking such trees as alders, quaking aspen, and yellow birch for food and building supplies. Some years, floods have washed them out, overwhelming dams and making the beavers very busy indeed. But above all else, their construction leads to an accumulation of water, which they depend on to define their estate. It also allows them easy travel and gives them a moat surrounding their current house.

Waking early one June morning, I start to read Beaversprite, which describes Hope Buyukmihci's efforts to build an animal sanctuary. The text transports me so far out of myself that Sandy has to yell in my good ear to get my attention.

"Want to go check out the island for beaver?"

Since early morning is a good time to go, we sneak…step by step…toward the pond, hoping our new camouflage pants and shirts will keep us invisible. Sandy stops and points. We freeze. A beaver is still at work, apparently unaware that we are spying on him. He dives, and we watch bubbles disturb the water while he searches below. When he surfaces, he brings up a muddy stump that he pushes ahead of him. As I hold my breath and pray the mosquito circling my nose will fly away, he tilts his tail like a rudder and seems to consider just where on the dam to dump his load. Then he hauls himself up on the branchy barrier, setting the stump into place. Without wasting a minute, he's back in the water again, slipping from view.

When he doesn't reappear, we relax. I come back to myself and chase off the mosquito. I had been concentrating so hard on the beaver that it felt as if I had become the beaver; that my human form had become transparent. I shiver with excitement. Sandy clears his throat of a tickle that's been building as he tried to be completely quiet.

"What good building," I whisper.

"Was that a male or female?" wonders Sandy.

"I bet male, and mama's back at the house with the babies," I reply.

While we ponder the unknowable, Sandy checks out the small mud beach where otters have sometimes rolled and left behind fishy scat.

"Hey, look," he calls excitedly, pointing to a small pile of mucky debris. "A beaver scent mound!"

We know we've found treasure, when he carefully leans low to get a whiff. "It's gotta be…Has that barnyardy smell." We had read how beavers are armed with a special anal gland that secretes a smelly compound called castoreum, which they use to mark their homestead's territory.

We have admired the innate building skills of these animals and envied their ability to build and maintain lodges and dams. Knowing little about house construction ourselves, we struggle when we need to repair this old house where nothing fits right and none of the corners are square. Just as the beavers tune into seasonal change when it comes to lodge building, we know we must winterize the upstairs so we will burn less wood. Since we also yearn to expand out of our two downstairs rooms, Sandy asks builder Murray for advice.

Before we can renovate, we have to demolish! Instead of mimicking the porcupine's lonely porch post feed, we throw a demolition party. One hot June morning Bonnie and Murray arrive with friends, intent on gutting the upstairs. After removing the two small southside windows, the demolition crew dons respirators, the generator roars to life to run a fan, and debris starts flying. Plaster crashes. Lathes splinter as they are pulled out of walls and thrown out windows. White dust clouds the air. In the melee, Sandy receives a direct hit on an arm from splinter shrapnel. Wounded, he creeps down the plaster-filled stairs to join the ground crew removing nails and separating lathes into a kindling pile and boards into recycle or firewood piles.

By noon, both the second floor and stairwell are clogged with old plaster, which the crew shovels out the front door or tosses out a window into the back of the pickup truck. Dust spreads everywhere. We escape with our crew to picnic and cruise in a rented boat on Lake George, grateful for our larger community ties that brought help all the way from Rhode Island.

Once cleaned up, all that space upstairs demands attention. We creak up the steep stairs and amble into all the corners, peering here and there, debating where new walls and ceiling should go.

"Let's put a wall here…and there…How about a toilet space in that corner?" I suggest. Sandy considers.

"Well, or maybe a toilet space at the top of the stairs, and a closet wall over there toward the front of the bat room."

By the next day when we again walk around, Sandy has switched over to my ideas, and I to his. Decision making has always been hard for us. I like to mull over an idea, chew on it, look at it from all angles, and yea and nay it until I am really sure. He quickly assesses an issue, comes to a decision, and moves on, not happy to keep reconsidering it.

Finally, a vision we can agree on emerges. Sandy then oversees the makeover, learning old house renovation on the job (with Murray just a phone call away—when the phone works). I hold pieces of rigid insulation that Sandy cuts with a handsaw. Some fit just right; others make him cuss. Then he cuts pine board after pine board and nails them onto walls and ceiling. Months later we celebrate the new layout: two bedrooms, a storage closet, and a toilet alcove. Ours. The old house now feels like home.

Of course, it really isn't ours. Even though we have claimed our territory we share it, for there are others who have staked a claim here, too. Some, like the skittering field mice, who are particularly lured to this shelter as days get cold, are as unwelcome as the porcupine. These cute animals don't tear down the house, but their habits of chewing and nibbling and leaving behind feces, potentially laden with deadly hanta virus, make us leery of them.

Now that we sleep upstairs, we hear their nightly travels. Swathed in darkness, we listen as the invaders scramble inside the wall next to the bed, moving noisily up into the crawlspace over our heads. There the sounds cease suddenly, as cheese-baited traps turn the attic into killing fields. I sigh and turn my deaf ear up, trying not to listen, as I close my eyes, appalled that these deaths are necessary to make our life here feasible.

Fortunately, we are learning to live with other wild creatures. We even consider them good neighbors. Spiders guard the single pane windows where their sticky webs capture black flies and mosquitoes. They also feast on the tiresome buzzing cluster flies that spend their winter with us. In the summer we welcome the little brown bats who still flutter off at dusk and return at dawn on mosquito patrol. I have rebelled when they have tried to join us inside the house. Waking to the slight sounds of something fluttering around the room, I nudge Sandy. He yawns and flips the flashlight on a bat, unhappily flinging itself from wall to wall. My reflex reaction is to dive under the blanket, my body positive the bat is after me, while my brain looks on, askance. Sandy rushes downstairs and returns with a butterfly net, which he uses to carefully capture the bat and release it out the front door.

Knowing they like a warm, dark roost for daylight snoozing, Sandy built them a bat house out of wood scraps, and attached it to the south gable of the house. Nevertheless, they mostly have been happy to call the cracks and crevices around the slate roofline and chimney their home until cold weather induces them to move north ten miles where we think they winter in abandoned graphite mines.

The garter snakes who hang out in the foundation and the ladybugs who winter upstairs inside the south-facing wall don't pay rent, but they offer such services as rodent and insect control. Sometimes we find snake skins which give me pause, for surely we are also shedding our former lives as the months go by. Where will I find them discarded?

As I drift back to sleep I realize this house doesn't belong to us alone; it is our house to share. As we evolve into homesteaders, we can't just sit on the sidelines, uninvolved observers. Living here may mean displacing others. I hope we can use our powers to do this carefully, to figure out how to live with the incorrigibles as well as our more congenial housemates. One way or another, all of us call Journey's End home.

Try to pick out one piece of the universe

to study in isolation

and you discover you are connected to everything else...

like bits of color in a painting,

each of us a point of light,

our own coloration affected by all the surrounding hues.

Gary Kowalski, *The Ultimate Canvas*

Neighbors

On a wintry March morning they arrive. When I glance out a living room window, there they are: five sisters sidling under the big apple tree, stabbing frozen apples that the cold wind has dislodged onto the snow. These wild turkeys' pink, vulture-like heads wear beards, and their bodies seem cloaked in feathery shawls that glisten in a rainbow of colors. Seeing this unusual band of gypsies I hurry into the kitchen and beckon for Sandy to come.

By the time we get back to the window, the ladies are leaving, step-stepping one after the other across the snow-draped gardens and off into the forest that grips the land as it rises steep and steeper into the hills behind the house. We think of these uplands as the wilds that surround the more tamed valley. To the turkeys the uplands are just part of their home territory, and the frozen wizened apples fallen off "our" tree, are theirs for the taking.

This house and its attached woodshed and porch serve as a blind from which we spy on wildlife. Wanting to attract birds, we have hung two sunflower seed feeders. One was used by Sandy's mother at their house in town. A second Sandy made, nailing together odd pieces of wood and attaching a sloping roof board to give more protection from cold winds and snow. He strung these from branches high in the two tall sugar maples that his dad planted out front in the 1950s.

Our seed donations attract puffs of chickadees, and sprinkles of gold finches, nuthatches, purple finches, and brazen blue jays. Tiny downy woodpeckers, and their larger cousins, the hairies, also come. Chirring evening grosbeaks, snazzy in gold and black, retreat here from Canada for the winter and attack the seeds with gusto. One day their dining was interrupted by a golden-eyed hawk with a streaked tail. Its arrival sent the birds helter-skelter, scattering away from talons intent on a bird dinner.

After dark, scampering mice and squabbling raccoons show up seeking seeds, too. It is the squirrels, however, who try to monopolize the feeders. To discourage them Sandy slid slippery pieces of aluminum stove pipe around the trees and nailed them below the feeders. Squirrel acrobatics entertain us when they attempt to climb or jump up the trunks. We don't plan to exclude them and have set a tray of seeds on the front porch. They can also help themselves to seeds littering the snow under the hanging feeders.

After I fill the seed tray on the porch, I crane my head to watch a red squirrel. He has dug an extensive tunneling system deep in the snow. After looking my way, he dives into the tunnel entrance, only to pop up again at one of many lookout holes. Then he's gone, reappearing farther out in the yard. Finally, he reaches the safety of a serviceberry tree where he chitters at me until I go back inside. With me out of the way, he repeats his route, popping his way back to the feeder tree, looking like a prairie dog I observed years ago in South Dakota.

Returning from a March trip, we crunch through snow to reach the porch, glad to be home. I wonder how the birds and animals, who have gotten used to our feeders, fared while we were gone. Nobody is around now, so Sandy unlocks the front door and we step inside. We stare with disbelief. Curtains are knocked askew, pots and pans litter the floor, and the teakettle lies upside down with its handle broken. A cupboard has been ransacked, and a bag of flour gnawed open. Papers are scattered everywhere. Stunned, we stare at the mess. Sandy recovers first, and quickly stokes the stoves so the house will warm up. I walk in a daze, cleaning up.

Who could have done this? Someone has been inside, for I find bits of scat, slightly bigger than a mouse's, dribbled across the floor. Not until several weeks later do we solve the mystery. A faint smell around the propane stove causes me to peer under it. There the gray squirrel lies, dead. He conquered the house, only to find that it was a trap from which he could not escape.

As March gives way to April snow disappears and the streamlets on either side of the house fill with pushing, shoving water molecules whose strident music fills the air. While it is an inconstant time—with winter battling spring's approach—one thing is certain: chipmunks will be waking up from their snow-time slumbers and reappearing to raid feeders. We will watch them stuff sunflower seeds into their mouth pockets before returning to underground dens where babies wait. These cute balls of fur also join blue jays on the hilly field just south of the house, where we spread cracked corn, in an effort to keep the raucous jays from monopolizing the other feeders.

A doe and two adolescent white-tailed deer also discover the corn, although it takes many days of peeking before we see them dining there in the late afternoon. Their emaciated bodies speak of the hard life they lead gathered under hemlocks during this winter's deep snow. I watch the big doe suddenly turn on the young male whose antler nubbins I can make out with my binoculars. She lashes at him with one of her forelegs, sending him dashing up the hill into the pine trees. A few minutes later, she thrashes at the young female who ambles off through blackberry briers leaving the corn to the doe. I holler through the closed window, realizing I am helpless to interfere with what looks like child abuse.

While we love to watch the deer, we learn very quickly that we and they share many of the same likes. We plant baby apple trees only to have the deer browse them to death. We plant strawberries in a patch, carefully spacing and mulching them. I visit them every day, delighting in the way the plants spread and thrust dark green leaves in a dense blanket. One day I notice that the greenery looks tattered and torn. Patches of new lush leaves are missing. Because I guess deer have something to do with this, I grab netting bought to protect blueberry bushes from the onslaught of birds later in the summer, and fling it across the plants.

With the leaves stabilized, I fondly count the emerging strawberries and keep watch as each one brightens from white, to pink, to red. I even pick a few, before they too disappear. When I sneak a visit at dawn, I interrupt a chipmunk helping herself to a richly red berry.

"Oh, Sandy. What can we do?" I wail. Chipmunks live all around us in woodpiles, stone walls, and the perennial garden, where they tunnel deep into the soil.

After supper we sit on the screened porch—strategizing. Outside, a dozen ruby-throated hummingbirds buzz around, changing places at the eight-perch sugar water feeder, squeaking as they chase each other. Their feisty antics, as they stock up for the night, distract us. All at once a female hurrying to the feeder tries to take a short-cut through the screened porch and catches her beak in the screening, behind our heads. I turn to help, but the bird buzzes into reverse, and propels herself free, before our startled eyes. Just then, Sandy notices something moving in the strawberry patch.

He jumps to his feet with a groan, "Achh…raccoons."

I charge out the door flapping my arms toward the two masked strawberry robbers who scurry off, pretty sure they don't want to tangle with me. It becomes clear that strawberries aren't worth the battles we will have to fight to enjoy them. Sharing crops is one thing; losing the entire harvest, something else.

During our first summers at Journey's End the deer pretty much left our vegetable gardens alone. The truce ends during a two-week sea kayaking journey to Nova Scotia. We return to disaster. Although the large garden behind the house hasn't been bothered, another patch has been completely harvested: cabbages, broccoli, Brussels sprouts, all gone. Apparently deer love these too.

Since our gardening strategy is based in multiple, separated patches, building fences for them all will be a major project. We have to do something though, for the deer keep right on eating. They nibble the pole beans and then wipe out an experimental patch of buckwheat. Sandy stalls on the fence while we struggle to find another solution. A dog? Scarecrows? Some kind of alarm?

Inspired by another home gardener a few miles north of Catamount Mountain who is sure he has found a secret weapon against deer, Sandy sets to work. Around one garden's edges he pounds in a few posts and attaches fish-line, making a simple but nearly invisible fence. He also adds dangling foil pie plates as noisemakers. Because the deer can't see the line, they mostly stay away. The new fence puts us through our paces, however. To enter each patch now means leaping over or crawling under fish-lines. I sometimes collide with them, necessitating much restringing by Sandy, who has a new title—line repairman.

Our efforts to deter them have not frightened the deer. When I return from the beaver pond one evening at dusk, I walk right into a young one nonchalantly munching sapling leaves. She looks a bit surprised to see me, but continues chewing, eyeing me just as carefully with her velvety brown eyes as I watch her with my blue ones. After a few minutes I move on toward the road only to find the deer has become my companion.

"Look, you can't go home with me," I say civilly. "Enjoy your sapling, and leave my garden alone." My voice rises and I shake my fist at the deer who decides to meander off alone. I walk home chiding myself that I didn't scare her more. Once deer hunters crowd the valley starting in September, this deer needs to know that humans mean death.

This summer we awake every day to cloudless beauty. Life seems different from last year when we had so many rainy days we thought we might drown. An epidemic of destruction spreads around us. Someone snips off newly planted cosmos seedlings at the edge of the perennial garden. When I check the vegetable gardens, I find broccoli heads pulled apart, and emerging corn sprouts, pulled up. A lily bud, just cracking open enough to hint of its coming pink glory, is gone when I next look.

Something's haywire. As I turn around, I realize that almost everywhere I look I see chipmunks. There—wiggling under evening primroses—one disappears into a hole dug behind a pansy clump. Others scramble across the front porch, climb up a porch support, pop in and out of woodpiles, or investigate the loaded blueberry bushes. Then I spy one atop a dense green broccoli flower—just ready for our eating. Chippie is devouring it instead.

Too many chipmunks lead us to wonder why. Something to do with the dryness? Perhaps we provide them so much to eat that they have more babies? Some imbalance has happened resulting in fewer chipmunk-eaters? Whatever the reason, Sandy decides to take action and grabs three small metal Have-A-Heart traps. After baiting them with sunflower seeds he carefully places them: one by a woodpile, one in the perennial garden, and one near the broccoli.

Right away the adorable stripe-ies come calling. Even though the set traps often collapse leaving exploring chipmunks shut outside, we do catch them. Then we start driving. At first just a couple of miles to release the agitated little guys near a cellar hole. But they keep coming back. After removing thirty, we consider whether we may be catching returnees. Sandy swabs a bit of leftover house paint on their backs and we decide to take them five miles out to the main road near a popular trailhead. Though we never catch any marked chippies, we continue to trap them—forty, fifty, sixty…

We stop to reconsider. How can there be this many? Has there been such a population explosion in the entire Valley that we are just creating a vacuum that keeps filling up with chipmunks drawn from further away? Without a doubt—we are at war. We have now driven over 500 miles removing them, and we both agree that doesn't make sense. The alternative—killing them—stops us abruptly. How can we kill these friendly, personable creatures? The damage continues, however, with the entire blueberry crop about to be sacrificed. So reluctantly, Sandy sinks trapped chipmunks in a rain barrel where they quickly drown.

My first try results in the chipmunk escaping from the trap to swim round and round, unable to scramble up the slippery smooth sides of the barrel. I stare in horror at my victim, before lurching into action to push him under. Once his lifeless body floats up to the top I shudder with remorse, yet know I will keep fighting. The chipmunk population boom has turned these popular beasties into a garden menace and we can no longer live at peace with them. As I reset the trap and place it by the broccoli, I imagine I hear cannon shooting. The war continues, and I fear we have become murderers again.

Since walking sometimes gives me insight into solving a problem, I walk along the road, agonizing over the chipmunks. What else can we do? As my legs move, my roiling brain is soothed by unseen bird song: the trilling warble of a red-breasted grosbeak, the plaintive "Sam Peabody, Peabody, Peabody" of white-throated sparrows, the bright notes of a Baltimore oriole defending a tree on the island, and the cascading chorale of a veery. All tourists who spend only the summer with us, they claim territory with their beautiful melodies. Too bad we can't sing off the chipmunks.

I find Jim Grey close to his place, patiently restoring an old stone wall, one rock at a time. He pauses to listen to my chipmunk woes and scratches his balding head.

"Farming is war. It's you against them," he agrees. "That's just how it is."

While he commiserates, I pause to admire his craftsmanship. Everything he touches he does precisely. He rebuilt his simple one-room cabin's foundation, replaced rotting and mouse-damaged wall boards, created unique windows and put on a new metal roof. He's a neighbor we trust and depend on. I remember when his tree know-how and tools, coupled with Pete Gorrie's willingness to climb high into branches, helped Sandy safely bring down a mammoth maple that leaned precariously over his newly built storage shed out by the maple syrup evaporator.

Jim made a sign for each of his Wardboro neighbors a while ago. He constructed them from slabs of tree trunks that he varnished to a high polish. He engraved each of them with the homeowner's name and a bit of personal information. The signs convey the message that each of us is part of something bigger, where outlaws and thieves are not condoned, but the latchstring is always out. Despite the fact that Sandy and I are the only year-round residents, Wardboro continues to exist, with Marc Merrill unofficial mayor since 1966.

Leaving Jim to his work, I stroll on, my mind still puzzling over chipmunks, until I arrive at the Merrills'. Since they no longer are able to drive, we tend to visit regularly to see how they are doing. Today Marc greets me on his deck, where he stands staring dejectedly at his garden.

"Ruthie, look! They are all gone—every one of our beets, pulled up and eaten."

As we stare at the dark soil where just yesterday the small beets had thrust their greenery skywards, a chipmunk scampers along the garden's edge and another squeaks at us from under the deck.

"Marc, you've got to trap those little guys," I urge, knowing he and Nora love to attract wildlife to their place. They won't want to consider killing them. For years, they put out leftovers at the edge of their large flat yard and watched coyotes come to dine while he photographed them. Before long the food attracted so many voracious raccoons that the Merrills had to stop the feeding. Marc loves to tell about the black bear who tore apart their jeep going after chips and candy bars.

Our vehicles have also attracted wildlife, even though we have never left food in them. Our small Toyota's heating system was taken over as a nesting site by mice. Whenever we turned on the fan, bits of dried grasses and nesting debris blew all over the inside of the car and we emerged blinking, covered with grass. Expensive repairs ejected Ms. Mouse once, but she returned, forcing Sandy to patiently pull pieces of grass out of one vent with tweezers, until he found a way to dislodge the vent and use the vacuum to suck out the nest. More recently garter snakes have invaded the hoods of both vehicles. Perhaps their hanging out there is doing no harm, but when they rise up in front of the windshield when we drive to town and ogle us, we wonder who is in charge.

Promising to bring Marc a Have-A-Heart trap, I hurry home, marveling at the deluge of chipmunks. If only we could leave them alone and just wait. Maybe then coyotes, owls, and hawks would increase enough to bring the chipmunk numbers into better balance. That means giving up on this year's crops, which we don't want to do.

I sigh, wishing we could live with them as we do the beavers. My steps slow near the wetland pond where beavers have been at work. Ripples and then murmurs surprise me, so I stop to reconnoiter. Since we usually see beavers out and about only early in the morning or during the evening, I wonder who can be there so early in the afternoon.

Then I see them: two small beavers—must be babies—and an adult. Something has excited them. Close by I can see the poplar branches Sandy deposited, after cutting trees that blocked the Merrills' mountain view. I had always assumed beavers were silent animals, so the murmuring back and forth startles me. As the babies talk to mama, they help themselves to twigs that they eat like celery sticks. Meanwhile she dines on a branch, chewing round and round it, like an ear of corn. Soon the kits move on, and so do I.

Walking back to Journey's End, I recall how we used to take some of the small hard apples over for the beavers to enjoy. They had arrived, eager to eat. Sandy even got close enough to talk with one of them as she feasted on apples, before floating away. Perhaps she moved off to discuss Sandy's mumblings with other beavers. We stopped taking the apples and try to keep aloof, for we worry the beaver will come to trust humans. Every year someone traps them, even though I tack up "No Trapping" signs all along our part of the road.

Becoming silent partners with the beavers as they maintain their watery neighborhood keeps us happy. Fortunately, their actions have never interfered with our basic needs, and we try not to interfere with theirs. Unlike people, who too often tend to limit life, the beavers create a habitat that attracts many others, including: deer, coyotes, raccoons, otter, kingfishers, turtles, frogs, salamanders, fish, and muskrats.

I remember vividly the day we got acquainted with an otter. We were standing silently, looking around, when one swam across the pond and joined us on the island. The dark brown creature bounded onto land where he defecated and then rolled around on the ground. Again and again he bounced and rolled, this way and that, before he jumped back into the water and swam off. All that remained were the fish bones the otter excreted while doing his territorial dance. His image is instilled in our brains.

If this "beaver pond bed and breakfast" kept a guest book, the list of visitors would be long. During the spring migration we spy on mallards, black ducks, buffleheads, grebes, various mergansers, wood ducks, and other water birds who splash down, most on their way farther north. Although Canada geese have not stayed to raise young, flocks of adolescents come and go, starting in June. Today my calls to tell Sandy about the beaver family are drowned out by thirty such geese who arrive overhead, honking raucously as they circle the pond, again and again, apparently discussing whether to land. Just as I decide they won't stay, they swish down, settling noisily on the shallow water. I imagine they have joined the solo goose who has hung around the pond for several weeks.

By the time August ends, the flocks stop coming, yet the lone goose is still with us. I mean that literally, for mid-summer the bird (who I guess is a gander) starts coming regularly to our clearing, as if he is tired of living alone. Our cat tries to ignore the goose in the hopes that he may decide to move on. But he doesn't, and the bird's greenish bowel movements decorate the yard. He loves grass clippings, corn, and sleeping under the big apple tree to the north of the house. I learn that a goose puts its head back to swallow, and pants, with its beak open, on a hot day.

When Bonnie and Murray come to visit, Murray watches "Goosey" intently.

"That bird's got a broken wing," he guesses. "Look at the way it holds its left wing. I bet it won't be flying south."

I'm horrified that I didn't notice the deformity in all the time the goose has been a neighbor. Later in the day I notice a truck driving very slowly along the road toward our house. Looking again, I see it is following the goose who is walking right down the middle of the road. Surely, if he could fly, he would get out of the way. There is no time to see if we can find help for him, for the next day we leave on a several week trip. When we return there is no sign of Goosey. I hope he flew south, but fear he ended up in someone's stomach.

Sometimes people ask why we live off by ourselves. "Aren't you lonely there?"

In return, I query, "How can we be, when we never know who may show up?"

We do have an incredible assortment of wildlife neighbors, to say nothing of the valuable human friends who from time to time also inhabit this place. I savor each day, knowing that when I least expect it, I can make a new connection. I need to keep myself open—with all my senses awake—to the possibility.

Sometimes I wish we were more alone. If the hunters stopped showing up during hunting season, the snowmobiles during snow season, and off road vehicles, during any season, we would not miss them. Just as certainly as the chipmunks devour our crops, these human invaders destroy the peace and quiet of the Valley. It isn't easy to find the right balance, so that those who want time in the Valley can have it, without unduly interfering with someone else's desires and needs.

Coming to live in this wild place has made us aware of how we are always affecting other Valley creatures. Even though we may not intend to, our actions ripple off like a stone thrown into the beaver pond, impacting someone—for better or worse. We may be able to share the Valley's bounty with wild turkeys, and offer seeds to birds. We may be able to share the yard with snapping turtles intent on laying eggs in June, and garter snakes who call the perennial garden home.

There are others who are harder to live with. The number of chipmunks returned to more normal levels this year, but flocks of blackbirds and robins showed up to harvest our raspberry and blueberry crops. Just as a swarm of beetles may attack our cucumbers, and slugs take over cabbages in a wet summer, there will probably be another chipmunk imbalance that will leave us shaking our heads.

Being neighborly doesn't always work.

We choose to create waste rather than recycle useful resources,

because it's more convenient to discard things than to reuse them.

Even though those resources may be refuse materials with little apparent

value, such as the refuse of our digestive systems, when recycled,

they can prove to be both useful and valuable.

Joseph Jenkins, *The Humanure Handbook*

Waste Not, Want Not

On a hot June afternoon, I trudge the shady dirt road until I am stopped by a crowd of butterflies. There at my feet, a congregation of black and yellow swallowtail butterflies perch on fresh, moist coyote scat. Silently, they feed on this delicacy. Not even my presence disturbs them. Watching their winged vigil, I wonder whose lives fed the coyote that are now feeding the butterflies. People would shudder and pronounce us crazy, if Sandy or I snacked on someone's poop. For the butterflies, it is not dirty, or nasty. It is the natural thing to do.

Just a few steps further, near the jumbled remains of a farmer's stone wall I find another pile of coyote turds. No butterflies here. Bending over, I study the lumpy dark remains trying to figure out what the animal ate. That's when I realize the scat is moving, for a black beetle with an elegant gold collar stirs deliberately in the feces. This carrion beetle has apparently also found treasure. As I watch the butterflies and beetle labor over leftovers, I realize that in our own way, we are becoming scroungers, too.

Each day, one of us totes the food scraps from our mostly vegetarian meals outside to our homemade compost bin, half-hidden in wild blackberry bushes. When I fling apple cores, pea pods, and banana peels, or dump moldy bread, egg shells, spoiled soup, and squash seeds, I never know whom I may disturb. The growing pile of garden debris, dirt, horse manure, wood ashes, grass clippings, and table scraps is a popular place. Chipmunks, blue jays, or crows like to help themselves here. We hear raccoons squabbling over these goodies as we drift off to sleep on summer nights. This hodgepodge will stew until spring when a poke with a shovel reveals big changes. Only soil remains, ready to spade as new earth onto a garden.

In March I embed tiny seeds into dark brown potting soil in flats. Then I watch impatiently for broccoli, cabbage, marigolds, tomatoes, basil, straw flowers, and peppers to show themselves. When the leaves emerge, I hover, moving the flats to sunny windows until the plants are strong enough to spend part of each day outside. Sandy resurrects the wood and plastic cold frames given us by our elderly town friend, George Dudley, who has become too frail to farm. Each sunny morning we carry the flats outdoors so the plants can soak up the sun inside plastic walls. In late afternoon, when the sun has moved behind the hills, the babies come back inside to spend the frigid nights.

Near the end of April I grab the broad fork and thrust its five prongs into the earth of the large garden behind the house. Still frozen? Leaning on the handle I find I can fork the tines easily into the ground with my foot. After I decide it's not too wet, I start my yearly ballet with this quiet substitute for a noisy, smelly, fuel-driven rototiller. I limber up my muscles as I dance the fork back and forth, poking with my foot and pulling back on the handle to loosen and aerate the soil without disturbing its basic structure. Then I move across tiny Ed's Creek to the four small patches in the field to the north. The companionable chatter of the water keeps me company as I cross on the five-foot bridge Sandy made, using boards taken from the upstairs remodeling.

By June, I proudly survey the garden patches lush with plants made possible by the compost enriched earth. The crops we depend on to feed us in the coming year are thriving. I welcome the sturdy green onion tops next to the flourishing garlic, and get busy thinning the beets and carrots. When I step on my spade to hill the young potatoes, I notice the cabbages are working themselves into heads near the spreading winter squash. By August, I tote bulging bags of zucchini to town to leave with gardenless friends or the senior meals program. One year I bartered green peppers for fish at a small market.

All this largesse leads to soups and casseroles featuring just-picked vegetables, heated until flavors intermingle sensationally. Sandy makes cold zucchini soup by the gallon, while my quiche changes from broccoli to zucchini to spinach, depending on the latest crop excess. At the dinner table, we inhale the tantalizing odors and admire the rainbow of vegetable colors that spread across our plates. There is nothing like eating fresh, whether the crop is corn, tomatoes, peppers, or asparagus.

As we dine, these foods are transformed, becoming part of us, and we pause to appreciate them. At the same time we are transformed, like the yeast I stir and diligently knead with flour, water, a shake of salt, and a squirt of maple syrup to make bread dough. We are becoming different beings, valley scavengers who readily use the discarded to create something new. I rip up old blankets and braid their strips into a rug for the bedroom. Sandy turns an old metal barrel into a fire-box for making maple syrup and finds new uses for gallon plastic milk jugs.

We try to emulate Ralph Waldo Emerson's view that nothing in nature is exhausted in its first use. We are inspired by him, and by the butterflies, to reuse what our bodies don't need: our human wastes. In Massachusetts, we had regular plumbing. Water flushed our feces and urine away. They brewed out of sight in the septic tank which was visited regularly by a tanker truck. I tried not to be around when it pumped out the sewage, for it left behind an intolerable stench.

Research carried out in the 1970s suggests that human wastes don't need to be abandoned. In fact, if handled properly, they aren't wastes, but riches. According to a book about international toileting practices, there is nothing new about composting human wastes. The Chinese have been doing it for thousands of years. Once I saw a homemade composting toilet in a cabin in a New Hampshire forest. Its owner had proudly showed me his handcrafted low wooden stool with a hole in the seat and a bucket underneath.

"Easy to use," he said. "Just throw in a handful of peat moss after you use it. Then dump the bucket daily into a barrel outside where the stuff decomposes over time. Eventually you spread it in the woods." Hesitatingly, I peered into the barrel and sniffed. It just smelled like earth, and the contents looked like soil.

Coming to live in wild Wardboro has offered us the chance to reuse what we once believed were dangerous wastes. What we eat is provided through the energy of the sun. We want to recycle the materials our bodies don't need, and not waste the sun's energy. The puzzle becomes how to transform our excreta, to make it safe to reuse; to enrich, rather than pollute. The alleged magic of a composting toilet looks as if it makes this possible to do. Living off by ourselves, we can test it and see.

We find it takes a lot of experimenting. At first, I juggle buckets, one for my urine, the other for feces, while Sandy pees outside, concentrating his efforts around garden edges. He hopes his territorial mark will discourage deer and raccoons from trespassing. We quickly decide to call our solid wastes night-soil, for we hope we are going to produce, however awkwardly, new soil. At first we add peat moss to the night-soil pail, which we dump into large recycled plastic barrels bought for nearly nothing at a farm supply store. Once we paint them black, we hope the sun will warm their contents, helping to hustle the changeover. To my surprise, as I become better acquainted with my body wastes, I don't find this bucket work repulsive; just one of the daily chores.

Before long we rethink adding valuable peat moss, as that seems really wasteful. Harvesting this spongy, highly absorbent peat from bogs destroys wetland habitats. Since there are no bogs that we know of in this Valley, we buy large bags of this miraculous stuff, hauled from far-off places. We wonder about what we can substitute that will add carbon to the nitrogen-rich night-soil, establishing a good balanced diet to transform our manure quickly with little smell.

The answer is as close as our woodpile—sawdust. That seems like an easy answer to our puzzle. However, getting it is more complicated. Cutting firewood doesn't produce enough. Searching for sawdust takes me cruising past a lumber mill, miles away in the Schroon River Valley. When I slow down, a huge sawdust pile materializes, seemingly just waiting for us. By the time we return with the truck, it's gone; taken by big-time farmers to use for mulch and bedding. We keep hunting.

One of Sandy's town friends, Tom Conerty, shows us an immense sawdust pile left from an abandoned sawmill in the woods near his hunting camp. We return the same day, shovels ready, and toss the lightweight debris into the back of the truck. On the drive home, we talk excitedly, hopeful we are now well-stocked with this composting essential for the coming year. As the months pass, the decomposers do their work, and barrels full of night-soil and sawdust break down to become half-full of dark brown stuff. Occasionally, Sandy tumbles them across the backyard to aerate the compost and boost its decomposition by adding oxygen to the mix.

Once we finish renovating the second floor, Sandy is ready to improve our composting toilet situation. He improvises a magnificent toilet set-up in the alcove at the top of the stairs. It is complete with a flexible plastic chute which we nickname, "the crapchute." It deposits our night-soil into a barrel hidden from view on the landing atop the basement stairs. The toilet includes a plastic pipe diversion that separates my urine so that it runs into a bucket next to the barrel.

To make the alcove a private place, I hang a textured white cotton shower curtain on a rod across the front of the tiny toilet space. A bucket of sawdust takes the place of water. We quickly get used to flushing our night-soil with sawdust, and learn that the urine just naturally separates, following gravity to the bucket. We dilute the urine with water and dump this nitrogen-rich mixture daily on our gardens. The toilet's innards are a marvel, for they process our humanure swiftly, quietly, and without obvious odor.

Even though we adjust easily, brave friends who venture from Boston for a weekend find the toilet challenging. They take turns soaking in the bathtub in the corner of the kitchen, while we do chores outside.

The toilet they approach cautiously. Once they wave goodbye and their car crunches off down the road, we discover that lifelong toilet habits are not changed in a weekend. When I use the toilet, I note that the urine diverter hole is plugged with dark brown material. Sawdust? Or something else? Sandy, the Roto-Rooter man, pokes cautiously at the stuff and washes it down the urine pipe, impressed with how faithfully our guests followed the request to flush with sawdust.

On a landmark September day in 1992, I approach the composting storage barrels, armed with heavy-duty work gloves. Malta meows a soft welcome as she patters by, on patrol. Carefully, I clank off the barrel lids and start shoveling the dark contents into the battered red wheelbarrow, which I remember Sandy's mother used in her gardens decades ago. Then I follow Malta across the field, wheeling the rich brown cargo to the aerating bed I had just built out of layered branches and saplings crisscrossing each other.

When I unload the material and scatter it several inches deep across the branches, I breathe in the pleasant earth smell. This is fun! I poke a lump gently with the shovel. Breaking it open, I discover it looks like soil. Sandy joins me and we stare at the beautiful stuff.

"Awesome," I whisper. "Shit changed to soil, with no stink." It seems like a miraculous transformation has happened—the work of invisible neighbors. We merely have watched from the sidelines, offering encouragement. Nothing more is heard from the quietly decomposing compost all winter long, although its volume settles. Hidden from our view, fly maggots, earthworms, slugs, ants, mites, spiders, sow bugs, and beetles are at work mixing, aerating, and tearing apart the mix of night-soil and sawdust. Maybe even mice, moles, and chipmunks get involved.

The composting toilet is just the beginning. We keep finding other projects that make it possible to reuse something previously wasted. On the sunny, hot day that we run out of well water because we used too much on thirsty zucchini, we pay attention. Although the well refills in hours, we decide to save its water mostly for our drinking, cooking, and bathing. We tote buckets to the gardens from the road spring or fill them at Spectacle Pond Brook, two hundred yards north.

On a rainy day, Sandy gets a "eureka" look, as he stands on the screened porch watching the downpour. "A rain barrel! That's what we need," he marvels. "I'll put up gutters to drain the roof water into it, and we can use that on gardens." He drives off that very day to get gutters, while I order a rain barrel from a gardening catalog. Within the week our new watering system is in place. Now I exercise by carrying a watering can filled at the rain barrel to wet down dry crops.

I am also busy writing. Even on sunny days that beckon me outside, I sit on the couch with pencil in hand, drafting an article about a magnificent blue heron rookery that we discovered one day. I struggle to find the words to make the wonder of the place come alive on paper, then struggle to type the essay on my ancient portable typewriter. Hoping to send it to *Adirondack Life*, I stare at the copy in dismay.

"They won't even look at something like this," I groan.

"It's time we work on getting solar power that will run a computer and a few other things," suggests Sandy.

Although we've been researching electricity made from sunlight for years, building a solar power system for this old house seems beyond us. In fact, I can imagine us burning ourselves up. One day we learn that a newcomer, Bill Campbell, has built a solar powered home five miles away on Padanarum

Road. The next day Sandy is on our nearest year-round neighbor's doorstep with questions. Before long, with Bill's help, two solar panels stand like side-yard sentinels pulling energy into the house, and six batteries rest in our upstairs closet, making it possible to store electricity for cloudy days. Our lives are revolutionized.

Just a few miles away, we also find a computer technician who is willing to custom design a computer for my writing—one that uses little power. He even brings it to the house and installs it upstairs. We now have energy-efficient lights upstairs and down, a blender, a mixer, and a few power tools that harness the sun. I happily type "Rookery of the Year" on the computer, and send it off. Within a few weeks I find an envelope from *Adirondack Life* in our post office box. My shaking hand nearly drops it before I rip it open to discover my first writing effort has been accepted.

It may be the same mail that brings news of a new book about recycling human waste. After reading *Humanure* by Joe Jenkins, we decide to experiment again. We simplify our system, so that night-soil and urine are collected together with the sawdust, and then stored in one of four bins Sandy builds at the edge of a field. Each spring we harvest a bin, which has been resting for at least a year.

On this May morning, I approach the compost pile armed with work gloves. I cautiously stab a shovel into its dark contents. The earthy debris looks encouraging. When I dig out a shovelful, I find rich-looking humus, which I dump into the wheelbarrow. Once it is full, I head for the perennial garden. By now I am humming, really enjoying myself as I spread the new earth as mulch and fertilizer around the flowers. Stepping back to survey my work, I marvel at how intimate I have become with the peonies, lupine, and foxgloves. I hope they will stand taller and look brighter because of my wastes.

Reflecting on our human manure composting experiments, I see them as a metaphor for what is happening to us. All our Wardboro experiences stew in us, continually enriching our minds and bodies. I flourish keeping track of wild plants and animals, gardening, and writing in my journal, where I attempt to keep track of all we are learning. Sandy is stimulated by his retirement jobs: wood chopper, problem solver, renovator, and maintenance man. We are not the same people who arrived too early that March.

Living at Journey's End has helped us get to know our bodies and their place in the world better. We care deeply about what happens here, about protecting the wildness we have found. Reusing as much as we can, to protect both our acres and the Adirondack Park, has become important to us. We get angry when we see the Valley being misused. Too often, when out walking, we find candy wrappers, cigarette butts, or beer and soda bottles tossed by passersby. We pick up the trash, muttering about people who don't seem to understand that they should care what happens here too, even if this isn't their backyard.

We don't eat our excreta. We are not like hibernating female bears who eat their babies' feces or lodge-bound beavers who, in the winter, recycle their rich cellulose diet by consuming their own fresh poop. Nevertheless, we have learned how to reuse our night-soil. I remember the butterflies dining on coyote turds. The lives that fed the coyote took wing in the butterflies that day. Today, my leftovers are becoming flowers. All part of the way life changes as it flows.

Edible: Good to eat and wholesome to digest,
as a worm to a toad, a toad to a snake,
a snake to a pig, a pig to a man, and a man to a worm.

Ambrose Bierce, *The Devil's Dictionary*

Dinner's on Me

In late April, Spectacle Pond Brook is in a dither. Full of snow melt and spring rain, it plunges over falls a hundred yards from my house and chatters its way downhill until it reaches the beaver meadows that I can see from my front door. Here it wanders through ponds, fields, and mud flats before hurrying south toward Lake George. Lying await in all these watery places are insect eggs, biding their time until May's warmth turns them into larvae that feed and grow.

By Mother's Day, I know I'll have aggravating company when I work in the garden. Many of those larvae will have become flies: tiny bi-winged aviatrixes, who make stealth flights looking for blood. Drops of mammalian blood are all they need, but when they come looking, I don't give my blood willingly. Having lived in this insect-rich Adirondack valley for several summers, I have still not adapted to their biting ways. I also blacklist their relatives—no-see-ums and mosquitoes.

When I set out on a May morning to water seedlings in the newly spaded garden, I greet the tail-flicking phoebes intent on catching bugs mid-air, then eavesdrop on the multitude of birds who are advertising their territories in melodic upthrusts that fill the air to overflowing. I feel like singing, too, until I realize I am under siege.

Hovering in wait swarm the no-see-ums, pinhead sized insects who cut my skin, setting it afire as I water the broccoli and squash seedlings. I try to avoid their fierce bites by jerking my arms, shaking my head furiously, stamping my feet, and whirling like a dervish. All in vain. These invisibles take some blood and scoot. Their pricks give me a rosy glow and leave me burning and scratching. Even at night.

"Do you feel something biting?" I ask, as my husband and I lie in bed with the windows open, enjoying the cool breeze.

Sandy gets up to close them. "The darn critters are coming through the screens," he complains. Then we both toss and turn, trying to hide under the sheets as the room warms up.

A few days later, I cover my hair and ears with a red bandana tied pirate style behind my head, button up an old long-sleeved shirt, tuck my tattered jeans into my socks, and pull on muddy rubber boots. I think I am well-protected to prepare this year's corn patch. But I'm not! My digging disturbs black flies who erupt from the disturbed soil to bombard my face. Only last week they were living in the rushing water of nearby Spectacle Pond Brook. Now they do their biting in the heat of day.

"Whew. It's Black Fly City," I groan to Sandy, who is weeding nearby. I flick off the female flies I feel crawling under the bandana, tickling me behind my ears. "Let's take time out."

Only later, their scissor-like cuts, rich with neurotoxin, emerge as large, painful welts that linger for days. They turn my forehead into a battlefield. As I stare in the mirror at the angry red wounds, I wonder how this attack will affect my head's permanent residents, the eight-legged hair follicle mites (fondly known as lard worms). They, I'm told, inhabit skin glands around my nose, eyes, and eyebrows as well as hair follicles in my scalp. These microscopic creatures, who anonymously clean me up by eating dead cells, remind me of my connections to everything else. I am definitely not an island unto myself.

I return after lunch wearing armor. Pulling protective netting out of its pocket in my blue baseball cap, I set the hat on my head and awkwardly drape myself from scalp to chest with the net's filmy barrier. Even when I use this, a fly can still infiltrate for a bit of blood, but the hordes are deflected.

By late June I can garden in peace. Then the black flies have finished their egg laying and bloodletting. Because I may find ladybug beetles, phoebes, flycatchers, and swallows on a garden bug and worm hunt, I intentionally avoid using poisons to protect our crops. Later in the summer Sandy will prowl the yard and gardens flicking Japanese beetles into a dish of soapy water. Today I patrol cucumber and squash seedlings alert for fly-by beetles. It's a race between their escape skills and my squishing fingers.

At the potato patch I bend and poke, hunting for potato bugs or their orange egg masses. This early in the summer I won't find the fat larvae whose appetites can devastate the entire crop's leaves if we don't pay attention. It's their hunger against ours. On the other hand, secreted in the soil, too miniscule for my eyes to see, bacteria are farming our fields too. Their activities leave behind rich residues. Their hunger benefits ours.

Later when I take a walk on the woods road, squads of ferocious deer fly females show up, newly launched from beaver pond shallows. As I hustle along swinging my arms, watching dragonflies zip past inhaling insects, it doesn't take long before my bug suit—jeans, long shirt, and hat—makes me sweat. That draws deer flies the way a red flag lures a bull. After one fly dive-bombs my moist neck and nicks it sharply, I swat her before she can get away. This tattoo artist still leaves her itchy mark behind. Sandy has learned to defend himself on his road runs. The sticky deer fly patch he puts on the back of his blue baseball cap sometimes attracts as many as forty-seven flies, who die stuck to the patch.

I have learned that all these females want is a little blood for their babies. Just some protein so they can lay eggs. Strolling along the road, waving a maple branch to brush away flies, I consider my own three adult children. They were delivered from the watery world of my womb so many years ago. I wasn't a vegetarian then. When I nursed each of them briefly I never thought about the animals I ate that helped me nourish my infants. This makes flies look downright economical. A drop of blood versus the life of a chicken, turkey, pig, or cow.

I pause beside a shallow dark pool and imagine the river of blood I will donate to insects during my lifetime. Frowning, I shake my head to disturb the whining female mosquitoes who suddenly swarm around me, ready to pierce my ears if I will only hold still. I leave that fly and mosquito birthplace in a hurry, slapping as I go, intent on outrunning these uninvited diners. I'm thankful that by nightfall brown bats will swoop down here, to feast on mosquitoes. I wonder what attracts these hungry insects to me. From their vantage, am I an irresistible lure, a cauldron of warm blood that exists solely for their frantic feeding?

Summer slides into fall, and these annoying companions are gone and forgotten. It's not until we make a February trip to tropical Belize as public health volunteers that I learn Adirondack bloodsuckers are no match for their tropical kin.

During a visit to the Cockscomb Wildlife Preserve, I find a vibrant stew of bright flowers, gigantic trees, clinging vines, crawling lizards, roaring howler monkeys, barking jaguars, caroling birds, and, above all else, insects. No-see-ums prickle, chiggers leave itchy welts, and mosquitoes dance close to lance my hairline.

Standing beneath a mammoth ceiba tree, I watch large chestnut and black oropendola birds move around their hanging "basket" nests. Giant cowbirds lay eggs there too, before skedaddling to let the oropendola mamas brood both the oropendola and cowbird fledglings in the colony of seventy-five bulbous nests. The cowbird chicks groom the baby oropendolas, relishing the tasty botfly larvae that emerge from eggs laid by buzzing botfly mothers on the new hatchlings. This cowbird dining rescues the oropendolas from worms that burrow into the tiny birds, often killing them. I scratch two mosquito bites and stretch my neck, trying to peer at the feasting going on high above me.

Two weeks later, preparing to leave Belize after a month of weighing babies and filling out their growth charts, I regret leaving the well-baby clinic. Here I've spoken halting Spanish to mothers breast-feeding while waiting on wooden benches, listened to infants screech as vaccination needles punctured flesh, and smiled at toddlers dressed in cherished elegance for clinic day. I realize I am no longer just an observer. I can now haggle successfully in the market and have learned how to ride the local bus back to our cabin in a hillside orchard. And those mosquito bite bumps persist on the edge of my scalp.

The flight back brings us into the bleak black and white of a New York winter day. The ever-growing green landscape of the tropics becomes a memory. As I adjust to freezing temperatures and stomp our woods collecting maple sap to boil into syrup, all seems normal. And yet, it's not. On the back of my head, two bumps grow more hill-like every day. They bother me enough that I drive the thirty miles to Glens Falls to have a doctor familiar with the tropics take a look.

"Possible botfly larvae." Dr. Leach, fresh from a regular trip to Guatemala, explains that he took a botfly worm from the skin of another woman who had visited Belize. "There's always a hole because the buggers have to breathe." He stares through a magnifying glass and pokes the bumps, not sure they have holes. "When they feed, they may impinge on nerves, causing discomfort, but won't do any real harm."

Not more than one per bump he assures me. I cringe as I consider the possibility of two maggots living off my neck! My neck welts itch, then sting. As my fingers explore them, I imagine them as volcanoes built around two circular vents. When will they erupt? Hot compresses ease the symptoms, so I swathe my neck with a heating pad and try not to think about larvae and what they might be doing. Dining on my flesh?

Wondering how I picked up these freeloaders, I search out a book on tropical nature. There I learn that botfly mothers may have captured mosquitoes back in the rain forest and laid eggs on them. When the mosquitoes probed me, these eggs dropped off, home free. My warm scalp nurtured them. Anchored by tiny hooks near their mouths, their tails serve as breathing tubes, emerging from the holes in my skin. They exude antibiotic to kill off any bacteria, which is why doctors have sometimes used maggots to clean out infected wounds. Unlike the oropendolas, my body finds them fairly good tenants. Makes interesting reading, but I'm not convinced I want to be personally connected to this in any way!

Since I can't see the possible botfly homesites on the back of my neck, Sandy investigates. He shaves the brown and grey hairs that curtain the bumps, and stares intently at them through a magnifying glass. "Holy cow!" he exclaims. "There are definitely two holes and they're bubbling."

Following Dr. Leach's advice, we decide to look for the invaders. The plan is to spend Sunday flushing them out. Vaseline on the cap of a plastic milk jug will cut off their air supply. An Ace bandage wound around my neck and head, holds this weapon in place all day, bringing silent misery to two maggots who had been living very well. Now I imagine them screaming in some language I can't hear, as they are evicted. I feel like screaming too.

As the day dies, the battle wanes. Ace bandage removed, bottle cap dislodged, Sandy peers at the Vaseline on my neck. Needing air, the two larvae have emerged. Each lies exposed, on the ointment. Tweezers prowl, as Sandy tries to pull them out. They don't leave easily; tiny mouth claws dig in. Two tugs. While I cry out, the interlopers are vanquished.

"Let me see," I demand. Sandy gently retrieves the inch-long, colorless, segmented worms and we eye the two of them there on the kitchen table. Not a wiggle. I shudder and poke at their remains. Which end is which? Were they able to smell or taste? Did they enjoy their meals in their subcutaneous apartments?

All this makes me ask who I am. I am definitely not separate from the rest of the world, when no-see-ums, black flies, deer flies, and mosquitoes find my blood indispensable, and botfly larvae and lard worms choose me as a habitat. Then, too, without my knowing it, my gut provides living space to a horde of bacteria. I have read that in my personal intestines alone, their numbers add up to more than all the human beings who have ever been on earth. Most of them support my welfare, aiding my digestion, eating what my body can't digest, and ensuring that my blood flows properly. I am simply their home and place of business, rolled into one.

Now that my botfly companions are gone, I don't really miss giving them dinner.

Although I'm just as glad they are only memories of the time I became an intimate part of a tropical life cycle, I also thank them for making me aware of all the lives that live within me every day, as I blithely, unknowingly, go about my own life.

As winter turns into early spring, eggs are again hatching in our streams and ponds. Before I'm ready for them, the blood thieves will be back, having changed from water-bound larvae to flies and mosquitoes. At least they just drop by for a quick snack and don't demand hotel accommodations. I welcome them as food for my neighbors: dragonflies, bats, trout, birds, and other insects. They represent the rich fertility of this place. The Valley as womb.

Photographs of Wardboro Valley

Dead-end Road

Distant View of Journey's End

Close-up of Journey's End

Hummingbirds

Close-up—Flower with Bee

Swallowtail Butterflies

Trout Lilies

Turtle Laying Eggs

Garter Snakes

Malta

Ward

View from Catamount Mountain

View of Catamount Mountain

Monarch Caterpillar

Life is a body: a unity made of a great variety of diverse parts...
The body of life is immortal. Its parts are constantly changing shape.
They grow and change. They 'die', but that is only the word used
for their changing into other shapes...

Mary Back, quoted in *Mary's Way*...by Ruth Mary Lamb

Recycling

Malta wraps herself around my ankles. Insistent. With a jump at the screen porch door she makes herself clear. Our orange she-cat wants out.

"Why don't you keep us company inside tonight?" I ask. She watches dragonflies swoop low, chasing mosquitoes across the darkening yard and switches her tail, anxious to be gone for her nightly hunt. She has not yet caught one of these winged predators. Knowing she will not be good company, I relent and the screened door slams behind her. Late at night owl hoots stir my sleep.

"Hey, he's close by," mumbles Sandy. Neither of us is awake enough to stumble to the porch and give Malta a holler.

The next morning when I open the door to let her in, no cat comes. We tramp through the rain calling as we search the woods, fields, and her favorite hiding places. "Here, kitty, kitty..." After each call I listen for any faint meow that might mean she is nearby, hurt. Only a dreadful quiet keeps me company, along with the fear that she has heard me but can't respond.

On the second night Sandy pokes around the yard after dark, flashlight in hand, unwilling to give up. When he focuses the light on the backyard woodpile, two bright yellow orbs stare back at him; the eyes of a large owl with ear tufts. It peruses the neighborhood, before deliberately, silently, flying off. This great horned owl is definitely big enough and stealthy enough to have ended Malta's hunts.

For days we keep hoping she will show up. However, that owl on the woodpile suggests we won't enjoy her purring presence again. We both grieve quietly for the cat who ruled our household and the surrounding wild valley. She had become a connoisseur of everything that moved: mice, squirrels, moles, birds, even a least weasel showed up dead on the front stoop. In one night's killing spree she pulled three bats out of the air when they infiltrated the screened porch where we lay sleeping. Although I hated the way she attacked everything that moved, I had to admit she was an extraordinary huntress who definitely left her mark here. I sometimes worried that coyotes could corner her, but never imagined an owl would end her life.

The owl's flight provokes me to reexamine my world. The attack is a reminder that the apparent serenity of Wardboro Valley is an illusion. Nobody is immune to death: not a feline huntress, not her prey, not Sandy, not I. The thought of dying has terrified me ever since I went to college, where I lost my faith in the possibility of an afterlife. For me, death means oblivion; no more me. These fears of a final erasure jolt me awake some nights, the thought of non-existence swamping me. Feeling nearly suffocated, my heart races, and fear grabs me in a disabling hold. As I struggle silently, I listen to Sandy's steady breathing next to me.

I try to understand my terror. Growing up, I had very little experience with death. Since I never knew any of my grandparents, it was not until I had to face my parents' deaths, when I was a thirty-seven-year-old wife and mother, that death became disturbingly personal.

One cold day in January 1971, my mother stepped from behind a snow bank, in Northfield, Massachusetts, where she lived with my father. She walked into a moving car that killed her instantly. The phone call had come at suppertime. My parents' live-in helper Barbara nearly knocked me breathless, as I tried to understand the message relayed by her familiar voice. My mother—gone? Killed by a car?

Over the next few months, my sister Ellen and I took turns traveling to Massachusetts to stay with Dad. I came to understand that it was better that Mom didn't have to watch cancer eat him alive. He hung on until July 1971. When death came, I was grateful he could escape all the pain.

My parents' deaths revealed more death. There was a skeleton in the family closet that I learned about only in the days following Mom's memorial service. Her sister Ruth had come from her Delaware home, inconsolable. Ellen took me aside one afternoon.

"You know about Ruth, don't you?" When I looked at her questioningly, she went on. "She went crazy at the cottage and shot and killed Grandmother. Didn't Mom ever tell you?" I listened with disbelief, certain Ellen was making up a story. How could such a thing have happened? Mom would have told me. Unable to ask my father, for he was so sick, I thought back to all I knew about Ruth.

I was Aunt Ruth's namesake and she doted on me. She never felt the same way about Ellen, who had been adopted into the family when she was four. At first, Ruth was a mysterious presence, seen only on infrequent visits to the Massachusetts mental hospital where she was a patient. By the time I was ten and my family lived in Chicago, Ruth amazed everyone by recovering from the schizophrenia that had plagued her for years. Before she was released to join us, Mom altered her nightly habit of reading to my sister and me at bedtime, and told us the story of her life.

I lay in bed listening, trying to imagine my mother as a little girl, and later a teenager, called on to be a big help. Her father had died when she was ten and Ruth a baby. I wondered what it must have been like to lose her dad when she and her sister were so young. She would have been the same age I was. The two girls lived with their mother and grandmother in a Cambridge tenement. The four struggled to make ends meet. I could picture their summer cottage on the ridge above Northfield, Massachusetts, where they fled as soon as school was out, for it was still in the family. The story had a shocking ending. Mom described how her teacher-mother had set out to walk to school one day, and was killed by a hit-and-run driver. That happened the year I was born.

Once Ruth came to live with us, her eyes would light up when she spied me, and I was drawn to this beautiful, if enigmatic, lady. Although she gradually entered the real world, got a job, and eventually married, for years she lived just a short drive from her sister in rural Delaware. My dad spent his career working for DuPont, mostly at its engineering department in Wilmington. When he retired in 1965, my parents moved from Delaware to an historic home in Northfield. There they could be close to the cottage. If Ellen was right, their being close to the cottage must have been very difficult for Ruth.

Not until my Uncle Ed and his wife Nettie consoled me, but confirmed Ellen's words, could I accept the story. Not until Ellen showed me a newspaper clipping from 1933, and I read it, unwillingly. Grandmother had taken Ruth to the cottage to try to help her over a schizophrenic crisis. Feeling threatened, Ruth had taken the rifle kept to protect the manless household, and shot her mother. Sandy held me as I cried anguished tears. Why didn't Mom tell me?

After Dad died, my sorrow grew as I sought to make sense of all this death, violence, and secrecy. I felt as if I were drowning in this onslaught of new and hidden deaths. I was so indignant that my parents hadn't trusted me enough to share Ruth's past, that I was unable to help spread their ashes over a Northfield woodland.

I was stunned to realize that when my mother made up the story about my grandmother's death, she had actually predicted her own. My lifelong vision of Aunt Ruth died that day, although she didn't pass away until fifteen years later. Devastated by her sister's death, she slowly slid back behind the curtain of her schizophrenia. She died in a ward for mentally disturbed patients.

I now have a better understanding of the incredible love my mother bestowed on her sister. This love became a glue that joined them, no matter what. It protected Ruth, giving her the courage to make a life for herself. I also understand that Mom could tell Ellen the secret, for she wasn't so important to Ruth. She couldn't take a chance on telling me.

Over twenty years later I am still struggling to accept death. I now escape these night terrors by squelching them. I push aside the burgeoning thoughts, as I assure myself there is still plenty of time for life. I face my feelings by choosing not to face them. When I yawn myself awake the next day, death seems a long way off. I hide my fears in the colorful changes fall is bringing to the Valley.

As the trees cast off bright flares of red, orange, maroon, and gold, and the temperatures dip below freezing, I pull dying tomato, pepper, basil, and cucumber plants out of the ground. I load them into the creaking wheelbarrow, and dump them on the compost pile. I know this litter will be unrecognizable by spring and, again, puzzle over the remarkable changes that turn this dead debris into something new.

One cold day I return from the eleven-mile trip to town to pick up our mail, with a bulging envelope. I tear it open, knowing inside I will find the Cooper family round robin letter. For nearly sixty years my father's six far-flung siblings have used this circle of letters to keep in touch. Now it periodically arrives with news and musings mostly from my many cousins, the older generation having passed on.

I particularly miss my dad's younger sister Mary, for whom I was also named. She and her husband Joe had pioneered in backcountry Wyoming in the 1930s, before they became well known western artists. For over fifty years Mary had observed badlands, mountains, and river bottoms from their studio-cabin along the Wind River near Dubois, Wyoming. Her artist-biologist trained eyes didn't miss much that grew or breathed along that stretch of the river. After their only baby died in childbirth, she and Joe nurtured their nieces and nephews.

Mary became an important role model for me. Cross-country visits, first as a youngster and later as a college student, exposed me to her love for all life. She coupled her art and knowledge of nature with strong beliefs in a world where everything commingled. She shared her ideas in the "robin", which I read avidly. In the last year of her life (which was one of our first in the Valley) I joined her for a month to help out. Joe had died several years before and Mary, after surviving two heart attacks, was struggling to live with a colostomy that resulted from surgery for cancer. Her upbeat approach to her body's decline inspired me. She just accepted her situation, and seemed to make the most of each day as it came along. She was not afraid of death.

The recently-arrived "robin" reminds me I have a pile of Mary's letters written between 1935 and 1947. Pulling them out of a dusty file, I get caught up in her vivid writing and realize I need to know more about her views on life and death.

Once I send on the letters, I begin to prepare for a summertime family reunion that will be held in Rutland, Vermont, where my dad's parents, C.P. and Juliet, reared their family during the first two decades of the twentieth century. When C.P. wasn't running a butter-tub business, he was out in the woods and mountains working with others in the Green Mountain Club to create the Long Trail. Following this trail, hikers can walk the length of Vermont along the spine of the Green Mountains, all the way from Massachusetts to Canada. Sandy and I adopted Cooper Lodge, which was built on Mt. Killington in 1939 in his memory. We have tried to maintain the aging frame of the lodge as a tribute to C.P.

The reunion brings fifty cousins, wives, husbands, and children to Rutland, along with boxes of treasures to share. There I find more of Mary's letters carefully saved. I get promises from other cousins to send me their letters, once I promise to return them safely. As summer turns to fall...to winter... spring...and summer again, I read and reread the letters. Not only does her life take shape before my eyes, but her thoughts about life and death speak to me, loud and clear.

"Resurrection was the miracle under my eyes this afternoon as I stepped on the soft old corpse of an enormous cottonwood, its body against the shore, its mouldering limbs reaching out into the stream... It fed the roots of a small thicket of rusty and raspberry-red willows, whose long scarlet roots dangled on down into the water below...Soft cushions of moss were spotted over the punky old limbs. Grass and iris were tangled among the willow roots, on the surface of the big old body as a school of tiny trout flashed in the mossy shelter of the backwater...And the end is not yet. A tiny cottonwood sprout was starting, too..."

Mary's letters put me in my place. She gets me thinking about the tangled interrelationships I observe in this valley. I recall the moist morning I walked out into the marsh and suddenly saw thousands of spider webs, highlighted that day by droplets of water defining their shapes, as if drawn by some master artist. I watched a moth fluttering, caught in silken threads; breakfast for the resident spider.

I remember the day a hummingbird died, trapped on the screened porch. I had stared disbelievingly and fingered his softness sorrowfully before Sandy tucked the small body into the shrubs by the stream beyond the house. While the tiny bird missed his journey south, his nutrients fostered spangles of orange jewelweed the next summer.

Mary's ideas percolate quietly in my brain until the July day that we hike the trail up Goodnow Mountain farther north in the Adirondacks. Blinking, I trudge from bright sun into the forest darkness where the tall verticals of oaks, maples, birches, beeches, pines, and spruces stand like sentinels guarding the steepening slope. Next to the healthy stalwarts, the dead and dying edge back into the forest floor. On the furrowed carcass of one of these old-timers, a new generation of seedlings sprouts. Nearby, orange fungus has taken hold in the old wood; its hidden filaments speeding the decay.

As Sandy and I walk, breathing in the pine-scented air, we notice the toads. Each bend of the path reveals another one plunked like a warty stone almost beneath our hiking boots. A sudden motion startles me. At the trail's edge, half-hidden by leaves, a black-and-yellow-striped garter snake swivels rhythmically, his jaws clamped on the side of a toad. The skinny snake seems an unlikely predator of the dumpy toad whose body measures possibly five snakes wide. Nevertheless, the snake definitely has toad in mind for dinner.

We creep closer, watching the snake try to fit the toad into his small but expansive mouth. Meanwhile the toad blinks and remains remarkably calm. With a lunge, the snake grasps one hind leg that disappears from view. Nobody moves.

"Why doesn't the toad try to get away?" I wonder.

Sandy stares, puzzled. "Has the snake hypnotized him? Or is he so terrified he can't move?"

"Maybe he is looking forward to becoming a snake," I marvel, watching the tranquil toad.

Reluctantly we leave the leg-in-mouth couple to head for the mountaintop and the panorama of Adirondack high peaks that spreads in all directions in the brilliant sun. While Sandy climbs the fire tower, I enjoy the view from below, still caught up in the life-and-death drama. Then we start back down, wondering what has happened to the unlikely pair.

In a few steps we find them, but now the snake grips both hind legs of the trapped toad. We lean against nearby trees and watch silently, time seemingly suspended, before impatiently stirring and hiking out the trail. I am certain that sometime that day, or that night, or the next day, toad will become snake.

On the way home the image of this life and death coupling reels in my head. Predator-prey cycles of one life feeding another surround us in our valley. However, we don't usually get such front row seats to these dramas. Now I can see they aren't just feeding on each other, they are becoming each other. Mosquitoes become bats, black flies…trout, trout…otter, and mice…hawks. The phoebe sitting on a fence post, flicking her tail sharply up and down is an expert on turning cabbage butterflies, worms, and deer flies into phoebe babies.

In June when female box turtles and snappers lumber up the road from the beaver pond, the raccoons are ready. The day after the turtles lay piles of ping-pong ball eggs in holes excavated by their back legs, the coons nose out these burial sites and feast on turtle eggs. An incredible transition from reptile to mammal.

One winter day we follow coyote tracks through the snow to the remains of a deer kill. Not much is left: a bit of dried blood, scraps of frozen fur, and an unknown body part frozen hard onto the ground. Everything else, including the bones, has become someone else. I try to imagine all the bodies nourished by that deer: coyote, certainly; possibly raccoon; mouse; fox; and raven; as well as tiny insects and microbial animals.

Looked at this way, Malta's death becomes an amazing transformation of cat to owl.

Probably only a minuscule amount of her was regurgitated as a pellet containing bone and hair fragments. It seems miraculous the way she traded claws and switching tail for wings and feathers. Perhaps, like the toad, she didn't suffer during this change. I have read that pain is useful for avoidance. But when it's the end game and there is no way back, pain is likely to be turned off by the body. Even my dad appeared tranquil as death approached. I like to think that may be possible for me, too.

As my views of death change, my nightmares become less frequent. In fact, I find myself wondering, from time to time, who or what I will turn into. When I stare out the kitchen window of our aging green-shingled farmhouse, the twin towering sugar maples planted forty years ago by my father-in-law catch my attention. I was able to help scatter the ashes of Sandy's parents under these very trees. Helen and Carl nourish these sugar maples that shade the house in summer and give sap for maple syrup in early spring.

I spread Mary's ashes in Wyoming atop trailless Terrace Mountain, where she joined her husband Joe amid meadows of wildflowers, hundreds of elk, and even grizzly bears. We hurriedly tossed her ashes into amorphous spirit clouds, and hustled off the mountain as a thunderstorm took over. It brought both lightning fire and a deluge of water to celebrate Mary's return to the life of earth.

Her words, written many years ago, haunt and comfort me.

"There is no death. Death is simply a change from one form of life to another. As long as we feel superior to other forms of life, death is a come down. But when we become confident that other shapes of life are like our brothers and sisters, the prospect of death changes…"

Malta's transition to owl and the melding of toad and snake on Goodnow Mountain reconfirm nature's great transformative powers, whereby death simply turns into new life. With each passing generation, life is born again, while death becomes simply a transition. Perhaps this is life everlasting; recycling at its best.

Everything is done in a circle...
The wind whirls, birds make their nests...
The sun comes forth and goes down...
The moon does the same...
Even the seasons form a great circle in their changing
and always come back to where they were.

Black Elk of the Ogalala Sioux

Seasonal Foraging

Three feet of fresh snow the first week of March keeps us thinking snow shovels, cross-country skis, and snowshoes; spring's seedlings, garden tools, and hiking boots a distant dream.

Stoking up at breakfast, I savor hot oatmeal doctored with our own fancy grade maple syrup. "Not many bottles left, you know." I hold up the glass canning jar half-full of amber syrup.

"Let the snow settle a day or two, and we can start tapping trees," Sandy replies. "Gotta use snowshoes this year, though."

Glancing out the kitchen window I study the birds flocking around the feeders. All seems normal. And yet, when I take another look, I see them: newcomers sauntering along the newly plowed dirt road. "They're back!" I yell, and point at the five male red-winged blackbirds who are checking out the seeds. Their breeding marshes, just across the road, lie buried under ice and snow; not a welcoming sight to these early travelers from the South. I know their women won't arrive for at least another week, and wonder what these guys will do until then. Squabble over territory? Gossip about their missing mates? They hang around the feeders, snatching seeds and showing off their red wing-bars until, as if on cue, they all flap off at once.

Later, when I walk the snowy path to the woodpile, I'm stopped by chiruppy scolding calls from the nearby gnarled apple tree. Atop its remaining yellow apples, one…, no, two…, no, three…robins balance, poking the wizened fruit with their beaks. I wonder how many weeks it will be before thawed earth will offer them worms. The next day they are gone, perhaps headed back south to warm up.

Foraging is a valley preoccupation. Every day, no matter the time of year, someone searches for something. Beavers forage for branches and twigs; deer for leaves, bark, and garden vegetables. Chipmunks hunt nuts, seeds, berries, and flower buds, as well as vegetables. Turkeys and robins forage for frozen apples on March mornings. Then they dribble apple seeds throughout the woods, payback for what they ate.

Also in March, when the sugar maples leak their sap, the foraging year starts for us. Regardless of what the calendar says, though, nothing will happen until the weather cooperates. Not until the days drip and melt, while the nights freeze and ice up, will it be time. Not until winter and spring are fighting to control the world will we dive headfirst into the sweetest foraging rat-race of the year.

Once we got ourselves settled in this wild valley, we talked about making syrup. We read books, and got advice from local syrup-maker Frank Dagles, who produces many gallons in his sugarhouse in early spring. We wanted to do this our own way, making use of whatever we could find in Wardboro Valley. First, we stalked the woods in August looking for trees with the distinctive sugar maple leaves.

"Here's one," Sandy pointed. Just beyond I saw another…and…another. I stapled a red plastic tie on each trunk, and we counted fifteen maples growing in a circle. I wondered if these trees, that had to be at least a hundred years old, were planted by Wardboro farmers intent on leaving a sugar bush for those who came after them. By the time we finished that day, I had tagged fifty trees. We needed to figure out how to collect their sap and turn it into syrup.

In town, when Sandy was a kid, he had watched his father tap trees and cook the sap on a woodstove in the family kitchen. The evaporating water stained the walls, and moisture steamed the rooms. Carl produced a dark, thick brew resembling stringy molasses. We knew from the agricultural census of 1875 that the original owner of Journey's End, Dean Phillips, had made 225 pounds of sugar and three gallons of maple molasses that year. Molasses was not what we had in mind, though. We pictured the golden brew our friend Frank Dagles made and hoped ours would look like that.

Since we didn't want to damage the kitchen, Sandy set out to construct an outdoor evaporator. He unearthed a rusty oil barrel on one of his rambling walks in the woods and hauled it back.

I glanced at it doubtfully, but he reassured me with a hug. "A fire-box! You wait."

He set to work on the empty barrel with a hacksaw. Many saw blades later, he had cut a square hole at one enclosed end of the barrel for the wood entryway. At the opposite end he sawed a circle where he inserted a stovepipe to draw the smoke away. He puzzled over what to use as an evaporating pan.

The puzzle was solved when we returned to Massachusetts for one of our infrequent visits. A kitchen sale at Massachusetts General Hospital brought us treasure: two large cake pans. Surrounded by people intent on buying huge stocks of kitchen stuff, we offered ten dollars for these two cake pan/evaporators. Now, we were almost ready.

After Sandy cut out the dimensions of the larger pan along one bent side of the barrel, he set the evaporator on concrete blocks out at the edge of the woods. He tested his plan: stovepipe into hole, pan into its hole, two coffee cans atop corners of the evaporator, each with a tiny hole punched to allow sap to drip into the pan. Then we studied how to collect. We bought a hand drill, and several dozen spiles and started saving plastic gallon milk jugs. They would serve as our tree sap collectors.

When the calendar tells us it is the last week in February, we itch to start. We set out loaded with gear: hand drill, tweezers, hammer, taps, spiles, and milk jugs. Grasping the hand drill, I frown, before carefully boring two-inch deep holes into several trees. This feels like a big responsibility. After I tweezer out any wood slivers that might plug the holes, Sandy taps in the spiles. To attach a milk jug, he cuts a hole in its handle that fits over the awaiting spile. Then we watch the containers, sitting perkily against each trunk, and listen. When nothing happens we sigh, and wait a few days until it snows—a lot.

"Forecast is for forty degrees today, with below freezing tonight," I call to Sandy as he shovels a path toward the fire-box. "The same for the rest of the week."

By afternoon we decide it's time to put out the rest of the taps. With two feet of snow on the ground, we wear snowshoes. I stop by the tapped trees to listen. Anything happening? The soft plink, plunk, plink of dripping sap gives me the answer. The trees are ready. Looking closely at the opaque bottles, I can see they already contain varying amounts of crystal clear sap. Energized, we tramp paths to all the tagged maples, putting two taps in several of the heftier old-timers.

The next day we go collecting. I am a newcomer to snowshoes, and stagger through the heavy wet snow. Once my buckets are full, I carefully haul one in each hand. Floundering over the partially packed trails, I head toward our storage barrel. Just when I think I am getting the swing of this awkward dance, one snowshoe sinks too low. Sap sloshes out of both buckets drenching my boots.

"Whew," I groan, setting down the pails and readjusting them.

This sap may be water clear, but it is valuable as gold. I don't want to waste a drop. This remarkable sugar is created in the summer months when a tree's leaves drink in sunshine and carbon dioxide. The sugar is converted to starch and stored in tree cells. Spring sunlight changes some of the starch back to the sugar the tree needs to support its summertime growth. We aim to steal a tiny part of this food.

As I bobble my way, I admire the ingenuity of trees who know how to make their own food. Plants harvest energy from the sun, energy the rest of us depend on. We access the sun when we eat the plants, or dine on animals who eat them. When I tip the buckets and pour the water-like sap into the barrel, I imagine it is invisibly rich with the sun's rays.

The next day at 6:00 A.M., Sandy lights the fire in the firebox and we take turns minding the boiling sap. We have learned that the sap must be kept boiling, but not in such a dither that it boils over. While on evaporator duty, with the sweet steam enveloping me, I watch the sap carefully. It's like babysitting a temperamental child. Add a log to the fire. I blink hard as acrid smoke stings my eyes. Add warm sap to a coffee can to dribble into the bubbling brew. Skim off the foam that builds up across the gradually darkening seething liquid. Put another log in the fire. The heat flashes at my face, singeing my eyebrows. Add more sap. Skim froth. Add log…add sap…skim…log…sap…skim…

By 6:00 P.M., we hover anxiously. I thrust a thermometer into the almost-syrup, wondering if it is close enough to syrup stage to take inside to finish. The fluid froths tiny bubbles and rises ominously in the pan. Sandy quickly shovels snow onto the fire. Wearing heavy leather gloves, we cautiously lift opposite sides of the pan and pour the steaming contents into a kettle. Sandy totes the kettle inside, while I follow with the thermometer. For the next half-hour we heat the liquid back to boiling and watch the thermometer. When the mercury reads 220° the syrup will be ready. I watch. Sandy watches.

"I think it might be there," I guess. Sandy stirs the mass of bubbles, and they rise toward us, like a flock of geese taking off from the pond.

"Two-hundred-twenty," he hastily agrees. This batch of syrup is finished. Or nearly so. Now we have to filter it, to get amber gold. Carefully, I pour the syrup over a paper filter which clogs with dark debris by the time the last of the liquid disappears. After filtering again, using a fabric filter, the fluid gradually drips into the pan. Sandy pours in more. The syrup takes its sweet time slipping through, leaving behind more dark stuff.

"Whew. I'm tired," I admit. But we still aren't done. While I rinse the filters, Sandy reheats the syrup. When it is piping hot, he carefully measures it and pours what now looks like liquid gold into canning jars. We gloat at the four quart bottles shimmering on the counter. The maples have taken over our lives. We will be at their beck and call as long as the sap flows crystal clear.

By early April, collecting becomes a different experience, with unexpected benefits. The calls of newly returned red-wings keep me company, while squadrons of Canada geese pass noisily heading north, high in the sky. I no longer need snowshoes. The snow path has melted, revealing logs, branches, rocks, and watery holes.

Trudging into the grove, I get a surprise. Suddenly, something moves. With a whirr of wings a wood-cock flies up from the leafy ground nearby and retreats behind one of the maples. I wait, hardly breathing. Then the bird reappears, scurrying across a patch of snow, where her brown markings show up sharply against the white background. Once she reaches the dirt and leaves close to a spring, she disappears. I know she must be there, but as far as my eyes can tell, she is gone. Impressed with her camouflage, I lug my buckets, hurrying to share this wonder. We both agree that she picked just the right wet place to forage for worms.

When the first week of April slides past, our maple fever cools. The world is coming alive. I want to engage the land, so long hidden under snow. I walk our sugar maple route one last time to collect the bottles and taps and thank the trees for their bounty. The snow melt fills the brooks, and also slips invisibly into the ground where it gives a wake-up call to roots. The plants draw on this essential liquid, combine it with minerals, lace it with sugars, to custom-design an energy-rich cocktail.

We hardly have time to draw in our breath before fishing season opens and our attention shifts to the dirt road. The folks who drive in, dreaming of trout or bass, too often find themselves caught—in the mud. If the muck doesn't get them, their tire tracks wallow through the quagmire of the partly thawed, water-drenched road, leaving deep ditches behind. Mud season! Sandy returns from his daily run, incredulous.

"There's a van stuck in the mud by the cemetery—a fisherman with two preschoolers." He shakes his head in disbelief. "What did the guy think he was doing, bringing those little kids with him? Now I've got to go see if I can pull him out." He rummages around for chains and his trusty come-along tool. Its wires, hooks, and pullies have helped him rescue many who have underestimated the power of mud. Joining him in the cab of the truck, I look out the window at the apparently dead woods.

I know they are an illusion. Underground, life is stirring. In fact, a revolution is imminent. In a week or two when I walk the road, I will find a host of perennials emerging from today's apparent dead leaves. Since most will grow from bulbs or swollen underground stems that provide a ready food supply, they can appear almost overnight. They have only a short time to bloom before the trees leaf out, cutting off the nurturing sun. Once I spy yellow violets tucked into their heart-shaped leaves, I know it won't be long before the wildflower merry-go-round is running again: spring beauties and hepaticas evolving to purple trilliums and white bloodroot blooms, evolving to jack-in-the-pulpits, and on…and on…

The truck slows as we approach the van, up to its axles in mud. Sandy knows just what to do and attaches hooks and chains to both the van and a tree. He applies force using the pullies while the driver revs up his engine. Between the two, the van lurches out of the morass. Off they go, with two toddlers staring back at us with big eyes. We are left to fill in the holes with rocks, and sticks, and whatever we can find lying nearby.

Driving back, we are discussing the gardening work we will need to tackle soon when Sandy sees them: robins pecking for worms in the yard. A sure sign of spring's progress. Then, as I walk toward the house, something flits past me. Startled, I give chase. A black butterfly with yellow-edged wings flies an erratic route across the yard. I realize this is a hibernator, a mourning cloak, newly emerged from hiding, its flight also predicting the new season.

My daily road walk becomes a treasure hunt. I reconnoiter the woods, checking to see who has awakened. My steps lag, for next to a patch of evergreen Christmas ferns I notice tiny spirals shooting up. A new generation! Now that I am paying attention, I find different varieties of ferns all along the road. While some people eat fiddleheads, I just watch them with wonder, marveling at how their biological clocks keep in synch with the seasons.

The return of the ferns also tells me it's time to harvest a few wild leeks, whose tulip-like leaves hint of their spicy bulbs. Using a trowel I dig up a few for us to taste, stir-fried. Most I leave in the ground to continue their miraculous-seeming development. For they know how to create flowers that shoot upward on long stalks, the frothy blooms offering nectar to pollinators.

By the beginning of May I am certain the days are getting shorter. Although I know this isn't true, it feels as if there are not enough minutes in the day to devote to all the lives erupting around us. New stalks and leaves unfold next to last year's dead rhubarb, and green pencils poke up in the asparagus patch, making my mouth water. But before they are ready to harvest, we need to stem the tide of green that invades all our garden patches. Readying the gardens for our planting competes with keeping up with the yard, as rainy days stimulate the green mélange of grass, clover, yarrow, hawkweed, violets, wild strawberries, plantain, self-heal, gill-over-the ground, and dandelions that we call lawn.

Before the dandys show their yellow heads, Sandy has his digger in hand to remove these foreigners that he says are irascible weeds because they are so hard to mow. I don't mind their bright blobs on the lawn, which is after all, just weeds with a little grass. Thoreau, who rejoiced at an abundance of weeds, declared they are the granary of the birds. I want to keep their larder full. For years we harvested bags of dandelion leaves, before the buds opened and took them down the road to Marc and Nora Merrill. Even though she was nearly blind, Nora felt her way around her kitchen to cook this delicacy that they liked even better than beet greens.

In early May I hear humming when I pass the perennial garden. Two male ruby-throated hummingbirds are jockeying around each other. Newly arrived from Mexico, they are looking for our sugar-water feeders. Their red throats flash in the sun as I hang up a bottle of clear syrup. Within a week, several females arrive and join the males at feeding perches. These white-throated, green-backed buzz-birds flick their long tongues into the syrup, lapping up our sugar-water nectar.

They visit the newly opened orange-red poppies, dart to the blue Jacob's ladder blossoms, and poke their beaks into blue, white, and pink lupines. Females hang out in the bleeding heart bush, hiding from aggressive males, and feed from the dangling fuchsia blossoms. They are our constant company for the rest of the summer. They nourish themselves in a changing flowerscape of purple iris, lushly pink peonies, multi-colored foxgloves, rose hollyhocks, and phlox. I think bee balm, with its shaggy pink blooms and heady perfume, is their favorite.

During June and July I become the earnest, if overwhelmed, caregiver to these flowers. Watering the flowerbed next to house and screened porch, I watch hummingbirds buzzing in and out of foxgloves. They don't seem too concerned about me. I realize they are the ones who are really important here. They, and their compatriots, the bees, butterflies, and other pollinators tend the gardens, continually drawn to floral advertising displays and nectar bribes. They leave loaded with pollen that they carry from bloom to bloom, dropping some here, picking up more there, cross-fertilizing as they go. They make certain they will have food next summer.

When I dig up such take-over queens as evening primrose and bee balm, I again wonder who is in charge. Perhaps it is the flowers who run the show. They set the scene and then await action by their subjects, the pollinators. Some prima donnas, like the ones I am digging, make sure their progeny will rule by also spreading underground.

The strip of land, tucked next to Ed's Creek, becomes overflow city, where I move those plants that get carried away with themselves. There they spread to their hearts' content, joining goldenrod, purple asters, ferns, violets and blackberries that have chosen to live there as well. I finally dug up the tansy that I tried to limit to a patch by the outhouse and moved them there, too. These strongly scented golden-topped plants are specialists in spreading.

Wardboro Valley has made me aware of how much plants move around. The Johnny jump-ups never grow in the same place twice, and the forget-me-nots that I transplanted from along the road, keep showing up some place new each spring. Of course many plants are immigrants, like us. Black-eyed Susans arrived moving east from the prairies, while Wardboro's settlers went west. The Susans now fill uncut fields. Buttercups, daisies, clover, mullein, yarrow, and dandelions came with the early settlers who planted them in their gardens. The entire Valley has become their garden.

Aliens still try to take over. We found garlic mustard plants in the wet area where the road floods. Apparently the highway department brought their roots or seeds when they deposited fill to improve the road after a washout. These tall green plants with tiny white flowers are grabbing land from the ostrich ferns. Whenever we can, we stop and pull out the invaders, hoping to get most of them before they go to seed.

By July, I am running around harvesting flowers for pressing. Into my collecting basket I snip roadside buttercups with their sharply indented leaves and a few pansies from the garden. I find purple-flowered raspberry florets with their maple-shaped leaves along the brook, and blue-eyed grass (one flower per stalk) in a field. I pick them all quickly and carefully. Certain I have treasure, I hurry back to place them between tissues and folds of newspaper. My press, two boards topped with six flat rocks, will flatten these beauties and save their images to remind me of summer when it has passed.

Craving a midafternoon snack on a hot July day, I return to the shed for berry baskets, past the large net bag of just-dug garlic hanging overhead. I know I will find what I want in our raspberry patch: fifteen bushes given us by one of the town teachers, Ted Caldwell. For a few weeks, except when flocks of birds steal these luscious prizes, we harvest a quart a day. Calling Sandy to join me, we eat, berry after berry, capturing their fragrant taste on our tongues and rolling our eyes at how wonderful they are. Not even maple syrup is as good as this! We used to forage on wild bushes that Sandy's sister had found in a far southern field. Now we bequeath those to the birds.

By the time hummingbird babies add to the tumult at the feeders, August is upon us. While they search out flowers for nectar, I rob gardens of flowers for drying. Frothy baby's breath, yellow yarrow, multi-colored statice, and straw flowers have grown from fragile seedlings started in the house to robust plants with a wealth of blooms ready to pick. Just beyond the bridge across Spectacle Pond Brook, I sample tangles of purple wild thyme and clumps of pearly everlasting with silver-gray woolly leaves and dense clusters of blossoming pearls.

I plunge into nearby fields that resemble wedding bouquets with their extensive patches of goldenrod, white asters, daisies, and black-eyed Susans. The virgin's bower twines its vine throughout, forming a halo of dainty white flowers. The goldenrod pollen powders my nose as I cut long stems of golden flowers to hang upside down in the shed with all the rest of the floral booty. Since they comprise the main food for bees this month, I harvest minimally, leaving the hillside still aglow with goldenrod.

Walking home with my hands full of flowers, I am distracted by jostling in the choke cherry trees that edge Kitty's Creek and in the elderberry bush that I planted. I stop to investigate. To my right, a parent catbird is introducing a fledgling to the wonders of juicy elderberries. Their possessive cat-calls suggest they won't share these easily. To my left, a group of robins are competing for the small sour cherries, making the cherry trees quiver. Sandy picked these one year and made jam. Since it was tedious work and the cherries didn't taste like much, we are pleased that the birds like them. I spy ripe blackberries nearby and pop one into my mouth.

"We need to check for blackberries," I announce to Sandy when I return. During our first years here, wild blackberry bushes crowded road edges and abandoned logging roads, and late August days were perfect for berry-picking forays. But most bushes disappeared, shaded out by growing trees, and now we have to wander farther and farther along dirt roads to find the thickets where the really big berries grow.

Armed with long sleeves and trousers, we invade the brambles. Sandy takes one side of the road, and I the other, competing to fill the most baskets with the ripest, most swollen berries we can find. For the next few weeks we gorge on blackberries. Ignoring the seeds caught in our teeth, we devour handfuls of these juicy black orbs.

In early September I cook up the last of the berries into a cobbler that we enjoy while sitting on the back porch, watching hummingbirds. Very few are still around, for the adults left for Mexico in August. I worry as I watch the babies stoking up at the feeders.

"How can they undertake this pilgrimage without a guide?" We shake our heads.

"How will they find us again next spring?" Although we don't know how they will do it, we know they will.

September means it's time to dig potatoes or carrots, and pull onions. I relish getting dirty unearthing potatoes. Searching for the hidden tubers and pulling four spuds from a hill where I planted just one small piece of potato seems like magic. I feel rich when I finish. Meanwhile, Sandy is in the kitchen with the pressure cooker steaming, bottling sauced tomatoes. By the end of the month, when trees start to flame orange, yellow, and red reminding us fall is almost here, he shifts to apples.

The old apple trees and their progeny are so tall and scrawny that picking their small imperfect hard-ball apples is a real challenge. Sandy leans the extension ladder high into branches and gingerly climbs aboard, armed with the long-handled pruner. First he picks apples he can easily reach and tosses them at me, while I either duck or try to catch them to put into my large metal collecting bowl. He then balances himself precariously to swing the pruner high into the tree where he snips off apples that hang almost out of reach. Apples fly around me, bouncing every which way. I lunge, grabbing them mid-air, or hunt for the rosy fruit in the undergrowth. After he shakes nearby branches, I find enough fruit to fill both my bowl and a plastic bucket.

Even with all the picking we do, we leave plenty of fruit behind for birds, squirrels, and deer. While these not-very-beautiful apples don't invite us to snack, they may mean survival to our wild neighbors by late winter. They also make tasty applesauce. Sandy, champion applesauce maker and canner that he is, doesn't even core the apples, just throws them into pots and simmers them until soft. One year he made fifty quarts that we stored in the cellar for our year-long eating.

In October, I climb into the truck and drive to the abandoned Norton place. Toting clippers, I tramp through the overgrown field to reach a tangle of grapevines that covers the trees sheltering the remains of the homesite. First I cut and pull. And pull, until long, unruly segments break off, nearly toppling me over. With the vines removed, the trees seem to sigh with relief, making me feel as though I rescued them from an invader. Back at the house I spend the morning sorting the captured vines and clipping them into manageable pieces, intently winding each round and round into a circle. By the time I'm finished, my back and shoulders ache, but I stare proudly at my seven irregularly shaped wreaths.

Harvesting the apples and grapevines gives me goose bumps. I feel as if I am walking in the shoes of early Wardboro farmers. All these riches come to us from them, and yet we can never thank them or pay them back.

Emerson wrote, "All my life I've eaten fruit from trees I didn't plant." Marc Merrill loves to quote Emerson whenever we show up with a jar of applesauce, or a bunch of dandelion greens, or bring his mail from town. Instead of reminding him of all the generous gestures he has made to us and others over the years, we just smile. When we plant new apple trees and grapes, we do so hoping that some season, after we are gone, others will help themselves the same way. Maybe over the generations it all evens out.

Once the gardens are harvested in October, Sandy forages in the forest for firewood. He hauls back trunks and branches and sets to work chopping and splitting wood. He is aware that the world seems to be dying back around him, as life retreats from the approaching cold. As the days shorten and chill, I pay more attention to the flowers I've preserved and try to figure out what to do with them. The hours pass happily as I immerse myself in creating greeting cards. Then I experiment with using pressed columbine, delphinium, iris, daisies, evening primroses, and roses to cover wall tiles. Clustered around one of the kitchen doorways, the ceramic flowers are always blooming, no matter what the season.

In late November, I cover candles with flowers. Later, I turn flat rocks into pressed-flower rock gardens, rich with cosmos, pansies, delphinium, and those evening primroses. Dried flowers, entwined as part of a grapevine wreath, make good gifts for friends. As I attach blue statice, goldenrod, pink steeple bush, and pearly everlasting to a grapevine circle, I pause to look out the window at the lightly falling snowflakes. When I add the last flower, I realize the foraging year is also complete.

The approach of the winter solstice, which coincides with my birthday, gives me pause. While I know I am a year closer to my deathday, I also have come to understand that I keep spiraling through each passing year. This is a comforting thought. The return of sap, plants, flowers, their growth and harvest, berries, fruits—is ahead, as well as behind. Around and around.

We need the tonic of wildness...

At the same time that we ...explore to learn all things.

we require that all things be mysterious and unexplorable...

We need to witness our own limits transgressed.

and some life pasturing freely where we never wander.

Henry David Thoreau, *Walden*

On the Prowl

Part 1

The mid-October chill greets me. I hurry along the dirt road, arms swinging, legs stretching, heart thumping, hoping to tune into the landscape. The white pines stand dark green; their yellowing needles dropped a week ago, joining the many-hued jetsam of other trees. Now it's the beeches' turn to shine. They are wearing gold, bright amulets to ward off the coming freeze when their brown leaves will shiver in the wind.

Sounds keep me alert. The crunch of my boots, the screech of branches rubbing one another in the breeze, the squawking of blue jays, the whispering stream. My pulse speeds, my legs flash. As my muscles and bones go into high gear, my thoughts move inward. My brain churns, generating ideas, puzzling how to start this chapter. Solutions erupt as my feet pound. Then I stop. Looking into the woods, I realize I am lost in my thoughts. I am missing this beautiful day. I shake myself, and listen to the sounds all around me. Grateful for the ideas my walking scared up, I continue on.

Now that I am aware of where I am, I realize I am not the only human being walking in Wardboro Valley. Deer hunters in camouflage and bright orange are infiltrating the lowland pine groves, stalking past the tumbled-down stone walls and cellar holes gone to birches, and moving up the forested ridges. Their flood of trucks and SUVs edge the narrow road, warning us that others—with guns—are now in control of the land.

A gunshot stabs the air and I stop. Not wanting to share the woods with gunmen, I turn back. I feel sad that killing apparently is necessary to keep not only chipmunks and mice under control, but also the deer herd. I force myself to drown chipmunks when they devastate our gardens, but can't imagine pointing a gun at a deer, pulling the trigger, and watching it fall, lifeless. I never expected to kill neighbors, whether chipmunks or deer.

Still, I am impressed when hunters talk about their time in the woods. Our neighbor Marc Merrill's eyes gleam as he recounts his hunting adventures. He remembers with joy the old days, getting lost on Catamount Mountain, falling and twisting his ankle atop Pine Hill, and spending long, cold days in the woods with friends, learning to know Wardboro Valley and its uplands like his own backyard. Another neighbor, Pete Gorrie, spends hunting season with his stepsons, teaching them how to meld with the land, keeping all senses alert. Although he gets excited when they shoot a buck and share the venison, he also glows when he comes home at the end of a hunting day loaded only with memories of his hours afoot in the forest.

I can see that hunting may be meditative for him when he focuses on becoming one with the woods. Wanting to have this experience, without harming animals, we seek out wildlife biologist-photographer, Paul Rezendes, who takes us on a different kind of hunt, in central Massachusetts. This slight, graying man, dressed in camouflage, settles eight of us on the forest floor to share his understanding of how to become one with the landscape.

"You know," he says, "we humans get too caught up in our heads and not enough in our bodies. Not enough in the present moment. That's where a deer is at all times. So let's practice being deer."

We sit very still. Consciously looking and listening, I hardly dare breathe. I try to pick up all the clues I can from the forest around me. People walking by on a nearby path don't see us, for we blend into the woodland. Then we practice moving like deer, with frequent stops to absorb the territory around us. Turning my head slowly, I peer past trees and shrubbery. Anything moving? My one good ear strains to hear any faint sounds not made by us while my nose doesn't tell me much of anything. Paul raises a finger when he sights several deer, but before I can find them, they snort in alarm and vanish. Whew! We all relax, and admire their perceptiveness. How difficult it is to think and live in the now.

Paul tutors us in reading the woods to find out who has been there. He strokes hemlock branches, comparing the rough cuts made by deer to the sharp bite marks of rabbits on saplings. Then we follow him on a scat hunt. First he shows us deer poop that resembles peanuts and raisins. He compares these to the "M and M" shapes of rabbit scat and the yellow-green tubular pellets of grouse. Before we are through we also find the boney turds of coyotes, and blunt, boneless ones of raccoons.

"Our molecules are scent marks," Paul tells us before we part. "An animal entering the forest meets smells everywhere: a rainbow of information. Even though we humans have a poor sense of smell, it is possible for us to also become much more intimate with the natural world, and when we do, we can join our inner landscape to the web of life."

On winter visits, Paul also shows us how to read the snow-covered woods, tracking creatures whose footprints invite us to follow. We return home anxious to try out our emerging detective skills.

Part 2

A December snowstorm blankets the Valley and frosts the trees. When I peek out a kitchen window, it seems snow has taken over, hiding everything. And yet, as Thoreau wrote, "Snow is the great revealer." We know that anyone who moves across this white slate will leave their marks behind. As soon as Sandy and I have paths shoveled and chores done, we are out the door to see what footprint stories the snow will tell.

Some are short tales written by red squirrels scampering between trees, or by mice. Their tiny tracks, stitched together by the thread of a tail-line, emerge from under a log. They accumulate to form a necklace that slides into a hole where the animals tunneled. Heart-shaped tracks under an old apple tree tell us that deer pawed downed apples there before moving across the field to the road.

"Let's backtrack them and see where they were last night," suggests Sandy. "There were at least two." He points to two sets of tracks. Lumbering on snowshoes we follow the hoof marks into the woods past the well, under low branches, between closely growing trees, more steeply up onto a hillock where we see signs of digging—maybe for acorns.

"Hey look, a bed," calls Sandy. The tracks he was following come to a depression in the snow, with yellow stains close by. We both sniff. Paul taught us this fruity scent means it is deer urine. The tracks I am following go up another hillock where I find a second bed, and beyond, a third. Just then Sandy discovers a depression under some pine trees. Two sets of tracks and four deer remind us how often animals walk in one another's prints, as a way of moving more easily. We do that too when the snow is deep, taking turns being the trail breaker.

I remember the deer tracks we followed one day, a deer thoroughfare connecting pine-and-hemlock-shrouded Cowbarn Hill to Northwest Bay Brook. As we clambered up the steep slope, using ski poles for balance, we found many beds and followed heavily-tracked foraging trails. The lower boughs of hemlocks had been well-nibbled and most saplings had been so chewed that all buds were gone. We never saw a deer, but it was obvious this south-facing slope was a popular deeryard where they hunkered down when the snow got deep.

From the hilltop we enjoyed a view of Tongue Mountain and of Lake George beyond. I wondered whether deer ever looked that far off. They are probably too deeply concerned with nearby dangers and finding enough food.

We know coyotes check out views. One early winter day when Sandy rambled up Catamount's ridge alone, he found impressions in the light snow cover where one had sat. He and the coyote sat at the same place at different times, watching the Valley below for very different reasons.

Coyotes make the lives of deer even more precarious. These shaggy, canny hunters compete for the same game that brings human hunters to the Valley in such packs. Since the coyotes are so secretive, we rarely see them, and are excited when we find their four-toed footprints in two inches of fresh snow on a January day. A pack of them had apparently milled around our compost pile during the night.

Lured by their tracks, we set out to see what they were up to while we slept. We follow one trail, for the coyotes apparently walk one after the other, placing their back feet atop front foot tracks, moving across the field and road onto an old logging road. From time to time the tracks diverge, and we guess at least two animals were here. Their path twists and turns, revealing how the animals moved under, over, and around bushes, logs, and trees.

Once they leave the woods for the snow-covered marsh we are glad to be in more open terrain. Our pleasure is short-lived, however. While the coyotes moved easily on the snow, our feet crash through air pockets created by clumps of marsh reeds and grasses. Relieved to reach the snow-covered ice of the beaver pond, we pursue the line of tracks straight ahead toward the far shore and into more trees. Crawling under low branches, we find ourselves in a glade where the coyotes checked out deer beds under the hemlocks.

Were they hunting? Was there a kill? We find no disturbance, no blood. Only a piece of uprooted fungus, left behind.

We are tiring, but our prey kept going. Their tracks lead into another marsh, around more deer beds before crossing a beaver house and dam. Then, the animals stopped under apple trees to sample icy fruit hidden under the snow.

After a two-hour sortie we give up. I wonder how long this journey took the coyotes before they moved on up Wilson's Hill, beyond our spying eyes. We trudge back to Journey's End feeling as if we have gotten into the feet, if not the minds, of wild neighbors.

On another cold morning when I am away for the day, Sandy nearly becomes part of the coyotes' social network. Awaking early, he listens to their rising voices, yaps, and howls coming from across the marsh. By mid-morning, his curiosity draws him away from splitting wood, and he sets out looking for tracks.

Finding three sets of prints at the base of the wooded hill, he stumbles after them, grabbing trees to help him climb the steep slope. He can't tell how many coyotes he is following. Once they reached the remnants of an old road, they turned right. Sandy studies the narrowing trail of tracks and guesses they headed toward a beaver pond along a route we often hike or cross-country ski.

When he reaches the pond, he tries to fathom the scene before him. The snow cover has been disturbed by many, many tracks. Slide marks crisscross the ice which is littered with broken branches. The coyotes must have had some shindig before they called it a day. Turning back, he notes that the tracks scattered as if the animals had divided into families once the party was over. Perhaps each group went off to claim its own territory.

A few days later, after fresh snow has blotted out the coyote story, we both slip on skis and head toward the coyotes' beaver pond, wondering what we will find. We move easily uphill, plunking our skis down to keep from sliding backward. Just before we reach the height of land above the pond, Sandy slides to a stop. He points to paired tracks crossing our trail. Then we follow, trying to figure out who traveled here. On every downhill, the prints turn into long marks.

"Must be an otter?" The tracks disappear over the edge of a cliff. We can see prints down below near where Sandy had hiked, the day he followed the coyotes. Since the land is too steep for us to ski down, we return after lunch, on snowshoes. Avoiding the cliff, we stomp downhill, following the tracks to the edge of the marsh. There the paw prints turn into persistent slide marks that cross the humpy land. They lead over a beaver dam, and along its base to a bank where the tracks turn into a slide that disappears into open water.

"This has to be an otter!" Sandy points to a pile of black, fish-scaley scat. Winter lets otters create a veritable playground of slides and water holes that also lead to supper. I eye these wistfully, wishing I knew how to live with such gusto in the world of winter. We are novices when it comes to surviving in the ice and snow. We lack the skills of the otter or the animal who left five-toed prints close to the marsh edge, nosing through brush and a pile of abandoned logs. Sandy had seen dark fur and a bushy tail flash across the road there recently, so we guess a fisher may have gone investigating.

Curious about where this champion porcupine predator may have traveled, we strap on snowshoes and head across the marsh. I follow the tracks without difficulty, across a frozen beaver canal. When Sandy tries to walk the same route, the ice cracks under him and he jumps back, landing on solid snow and ice. Now we move nervously, separated by the canal, unsure of the safety of what lies underfoot. Once the canal narrows near the pond, he tests the ice before putting his weight on it. Then, hesitatingly, he takes a step. His right leg plunges down through snow, into water.

"Damn!"

Stepping to the left, his other leg crashes through, too. Alarmed, he turns to retreat to where he had walked safely before. Now, his trousers are so heavy with wet snow and his boots and snowshoes so water-logged that he keeps plunging into the two feet of water at the bottom of the canal. When I reach out to give him something to hold onto, he nearly pulls me in beside him. Filled with dread, I stare at him. How will he ever get out?

Because his legs and feet feel like dead weights, he leans back into the snow, hoping to make it easier to lift his lower body. That doesn't help. He just gets his backpack and coat drenched. More water trickles inside his boots.

"Ay-yiy!" he yells. "It's cold!" He struggles to stand but he can't. His wet clothing freezes, making him feel even heavier. His boots, clamped onto his ungainly snowshoes, seem immovable.

"I'm not going to make it."

It seems my heart has stopped. He can't have said that! There is no one else in the valley to rescue him. Frantic, I cry, "Come on, you've got to try!"

"Maybe I can get up on the pond." He studies the look of its ice, ten feet away.

Lying on his back, he scooches awkwardly toward it. Then, slowly, he lifts himself until his upper body is on the ice. It holds! He rolls over onto his belly and slides forward until he can raise his legs. When I hurry to join him, I realize I'm shaking uncontrollably. Working to remove his heavy snowshoes, we find they are frozen onto his boots. There is nothing to do but stumble the ten-minute walk home. We are beyond words. "What if's…" silence us. As I walk next to him, I grab his arm and can feel him shivering, although he is apparently unhurt.

Once inside the warm house we peel off his frozen pack and clothing and remove icy boots and snowshoes. He stokes the wood fire in the big kitchen stove, enjoying the heat, while I putter getting the bathtub ready. Once the two large pots of hot water atop the woodstove are emptied into the bathtub and cold water added from the faucet, he takes a long soak. He decides he will live.

We are both humbled We will not take ice for granted again.

Part 3

Staring out the window at the marsh, so thankful Sandy got out safely, I watch Catamount Mountain, its ridgeline and upper slopes glistening in the sun. This Valley overseer, whose visage changes with the season, remains our constant companion. Our forays there have exposed its wildness and further tested us.

Spring hikes, when the leaves are still only tiny points of bright green and the woods are flooded with sunshine, make us sweat and take off our jackets. Although there are no animal tracks to follow, I quickly become a follower of flowers that lead me in circles. It is impossible to hurry on up toward Catamount's ridgeline when pink-striped spring beauties, purple hepatica, and Dutchmen's breeches' white blooms demand that I stop. My steps lag while I enjoy them but Sandy keeps looking back, urging me on.

When we reach a gorge, which may be the only easy way up past the mountain's many cliffs, I discover a lush rock garden. Purple violets have gotten a toehold on the wet rock and are accompanied by moss and ferns. Looking for Catamount's peak takes us on a long, roundabout hunt. We try to figure out a route that avoids trees, saplings, hobblebush, and boulders. Nothing is easy. Soon we come to a steep mound and hoist each other up and over rocks. Is this the top? No. The ridge continues, with another climb up and down. Here we stop for lunch at a lookout and admire the Valley below. Adirondack peaks spread out toward the west.

After exploring further and never finding a peak, we head eastward across the ridge, where the land seems more level. We can glimpse Vermont's Green Mountains in the distance and wild Jabe's Pond directly below. The afternoon is waning; we need to start back. On the descent, we hope we won't need to climb down one of Catamount's cliffs. Wishing we had brought a compass, we watch the sun and follow the lay of the land which luckily leads to the rocky gorge.

Continuing down more steeply, I realize how tired I am. Feeling my way, looking for safe footing, I nudge a little brown mouse or vole, half-hidden in leaves at my feet. As I bend to get a closer look, it scampers off to a better hiding place.

"Hey," Sandy calls from below. "Here's a beech tree with bear claw marks going up into the upper branches. I bet it was after beechnuts."

The bear claws have made wounds in the smooth gray bark that seem to have enlarged as the tree grew. Wondering if there are any bears nearby right now, I move faster, following Sandy down the mountain. After eight hours of exploring, we walk into our clearing. Though our muscles are aching, we agree that now we want to climb the easier appearing eastern side, to find the highest point of the ridge.

In early October, before the hunters reclaim the woods, we drive over dirt roads to the other side of Catamount, where we slip the canoe into Jabe's Pond. Heading for the south shore where we will start our hike, we paddle easily, enjoying the glorious colors of the surrounding forest and the antics of three loons who are near us one minute and hidden under water the next. We beach the canoe in a thicket, and grab our packs. Sandy has the compass, which we will depend on to get back to the pond.

We aim toward Catamount's slopes, working our way past an evergreen covered knoll to start our climb. Unfortunately, the route is tougher than we expected. Steep terrain turns to rocky walls, so we head farther south hoping to find a more reasonable incline. Whenever the climb moderates, we clamber upward, until striving to pull myself up over a rock I bang my knee—hard.

"Ouch!" With tears in my eyes, I collapse and tentatively touch the injury. After a drink from my canteen, we continue, Sandy leading through a tangle of undergrowth while I limp behind. Finally, we come to what appears to be the highest point, and we settle down to rest and eat our lunch.

"Can't see much from here." Sandy tries to peer through a tangle of trees, while we nibble slices of oatmeal bread and crunch carrot sticks and apples. "But this is far enough for today. We want to make sure your knee will get you back to the pond."

Climbing down the mountain seems pretty straightforward. The challenge comes when we try to find Jabe's Pond. We follow the compass—northeast—remembering we may have to hike over that knoll of evergreens. My knee aches and slows me down—but we keep going until we see water ahead. I relax, certain that this is the edge of the pond and we will soon be back in the canoe. As we get closer, we find a beaver-dammed stream—not Jabe's Pond at all. We check the compass and peruse the topographical map. Sandy points to blue lines indicating marshland.

"I think that is much farther east," he says. "But maybe that's where we are. Let's look around."

Trying to pay attention to both the compass and the lay of the land, we bumble about, hoping the stream will take us to Jabe's Pond. When it doesn't, we stop.

"Let's try going the other way," I suggest.

So we reverse direction. Sandy walks along watching the compass. It indicates that the stream we are following is heading east. Before long he sees we are now going north, and a few minutes later, west. My knee throbs and we stop. Sandy looks worried.

"I don't know where Jabe's Pond is, but we will just have to follow this stream. It will either come out at the Pond or take us down toward Lake George."

The sun is moving toward the western horizon, and I don't want to spend this October night in the woods. On the bright side, we have light coats, my canteen still has water, and Sandy has matches. On the other hand, we ate all our food at lunch. Because I worry how well we will manage if the temperature drops toward freezing, I hustle. Trying not to limp, I step from rock to rock in the stream and then along the rough ground next to it. As we move along, we wonder how we can possibly be heading west, but the compass continues to insist that's where we are going. The way continues downhill, ever more steeply.

I walk blindly, lost in churning emotions. One minute I'm scared because no one knows we are out in the woods, and the next intrigued. I wonder what we could learn from staying overnight here. I start to think about what we would need to do, when Sandy stops.

"Hey, I know where we are!" He points ahead toward rocky slabs that define the stream as it turns sharply downward. I stare hopefully, but it doesn't look familiar to me.

"We're almost at the rocky grotto where we've skinny dipped," he says.

We scramble up a mossy height above the stream, and I cross my fingers. Please let this be Flybrook! Down below, stone walls disintegrate into pools and falls.

"Can there be more than one stream with such a beautiful place?" I ask.

Our steady descent ends and we now walk easily along a low plateau that follows the stream. The sun has already set when we reach a sharp turn and recognize a familiar cellar-hole. I suddenly feel twenty pounds lighter. We stroll confidently through the white pines. Barely aware of my aching knee, my senses engage each tree, each step that brings us closer to home. We hurry past the coyotes' beaver pond, back to our Journey's End. How wonderful to walk where the landscape looks familiar!

As we approach the house I see Catamount, its slopes gleaming pink from the reflected rays of the sun. Although very welcoming, all I can think about is supper and bed. Lost on the mountain. Lost in my mind. I am exhausted.

Thoreau believed that it was not until you are lost that you begin to find yourself. Not until then do you realize where you are and the infinite extent of your relations. As I doze off, I promise myself we will keep prowling. For, like Thoreau, we need "this tonic of wildness." It reminds us we are not the only creatures who call this Valley—this earth—home.

Everything is always moving, changing, becoming, dissolving, emerging, evolving in a complex dance, the outer dance of the world not so different from the inner dance of our own mind.

Jon Kabat-Zinn and Myla Kabat-Zinn, *An Eighteen Year Retreat*

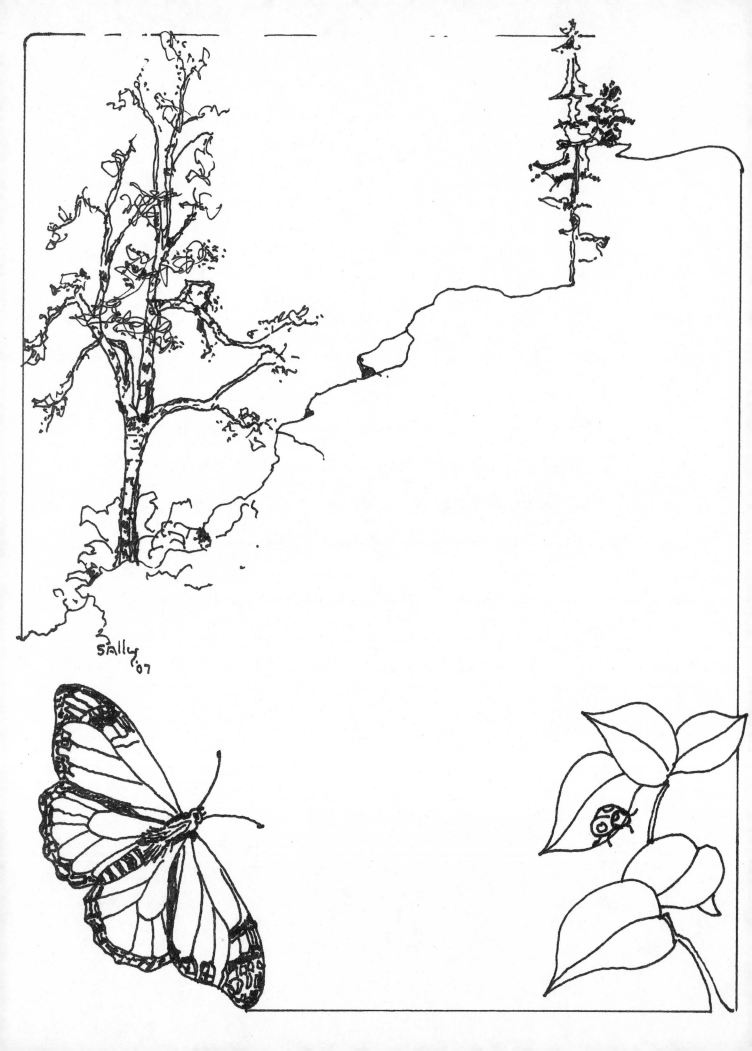

Metamorphosis

Logs lie like lovers, ready to burn, tickled by smashed newspaper. I light a match: orgasmic flames leap, feeding frantically, snapping, shooting high and higher. Brown to rose to black to white—a new logscape unfolds into a gray ashscape topped with swirling smoke. I lie on the living room couch half-awake, entranced by the fire. Its passion is transforming.

Intimacy has not been easy for me. Getting close might mean getting burned. I remember my awkward attempts as an adolescent to get a boyfriend. When it seemed he might want a kiss, terror gripped me and, certain I was going to throw up, I hid in the bathroom. Since getting close felt very scary, I kept to myself during high school. I got good grades and lived three miles out in the country. My best friends were my mother's horses. I built a wall around myself; I could choose to lower it, but I was always in control.

When I was accepted at Swarthmore College, an hour's ride away, I delighted to have the chance to be on my own. To symbolize the fresh start, I changed my name. Ruth-Mary became just plain Ruth, nice and normal sounding—even though this meant erasing my beloved Aunt Mary from my name. I couldn't drop Ruth and name myself Mary because Aunt Ruth lived nearby. She would have been devastated if I had done such a thing.

While my grades suffered that first year, Swarthmore allowed me to grow in new directions, including an intimate relationship with a gawky fellow band member—a trombone player—who seemed safe enough to risk getting close. Sandy and I necked in the college woods, fanning our passions next to the ceaseless flow of Crum Creek. We married in 1956, after his first year in medical school. Over the years, as our passions evolved to everyday caring, I realized that I didn't give myself easily to our lovemaking. The need to be in control had become a reflex. I still lived behind that wall.

Becoming intimate with the Valley—where I can't be in control—has helped me. The pulsing life makes intimacy feel very natural. Whether you are a wild columbine, oak, fern, mosquito, butterfly, garter snake, Baltimore oriole, or coyote—sex comes first here. Nothing is more important than producing offspring.

One of our first explorations led us north along the unmaintained road. We pushed ourselves up forested hills, crossing two streams on simple snowmobile bridges, and passing two beaver wetlands. In about three miles we reached a split in the road and considered our choices. Since turning left promised to take us to the glimmer of water we could see through the trees, Sandy helped steady me as I picked my way from rock to rock across a brook. Then we walked hand in hand along the rough track. At the edge of a pond, we stopped and stared. And listened.

On this sunny June morning bullfrogs brayed, green frogs twanged, and a pileated woodpecker added his tree drum. Tree swallows darted overhead, high above whirligig beetles, swirling atop the still water. Below, tan salamanders gyrated through the shallows. Mallards quacked on the other side of a beaver house, and the calls of white-throated sparrows seemed to wrap us in a ribbon of song. Sliding wordlessly to the ground we wrapped ourselves around each other, feeling at one with this vibrating place. All the sounds melded with the sky, pond, the overhanging trees, and us.

When ants tickled my ankles, intent on making me part of their world, I brushed them off, and we uncurled. Leaning against a log, we lunched on Sandy's fresh rolls and looked around. At the same moment we both noticed the big stick nest atop a dead tree in the middle of the pond. Then, Sandy pointed excitedly. A stick-like bird showed itself briefly before disappearing back into the nest.

A blue heron sitting on eggs! It epitomized the life brewing all around us.

It all starts in February when the owls court and the coyotes breed. Reproduction doesn't become obvious, however, until late March or early April when the wood frogs mate. On a sunny day, we walk through melting snow to the coyote's beaver pond, enjoying the open woods of winter before spring's green scarf of leaves veils them. When we arrive, vibrating water and knobby frog heads urge patience, until a few minstrels sing their quacking song. Then the whole choir chimes in, and two by two (and sometimes three) the frogs do their mating dance.

I notice a hawk floating above the tallest pines, biding its time, just before nearby yaps and yips of coyotes make me aware how hazardous these romantic connections may be. While some of these frogs may become hawk or coyote, I trust the eggs left behind will insure that a new generation will sound off again next spring.

On wet April nights we walk the road in slickers, flicking the beams of our flashlights on the orange markings of a spotted salamander crossing the road to reach a breeding pool. Without any to-do, a male will deposit sperm into the water which the female finds and uses to fertilize her eggs, all done so quietly in the dark that we never know it happens. On the way back we listen to the spring peepers, who carry on their courtship antics at such a loud pitch that I can't believe all that screaming comes from such tiny creatures.

April rains also bring a profusion of red efts, scattered so densely along the dirt road that I have to watch where I step. These tiny salamanders never seem to be going anywhere and yet they spend most of their lives traveling. After a first summer of pond living as yellow-green newts, they turn into brick red mini-dragons and head for land. They will wander for two years, flashing vermillion spots armed with protective toxic fluids. When I find them along the road, the three-year olds are headed back to the pond to change their colors again. They will breed the next generation, prompted by DNA instructions that tell them just what to do and when.

I marvel at such instincts and how they empower so many Wardboro lives. Courtship happens at the right moment, whether you are an owl, coyote, eft, frog, or ruffed grouse drumming on a log. The woodcock's specialty is his courtship dance. Nothing retiring about him, although his wives are quiet types.

Every April one woodcock regularly entertains the ladies and us with his antics. It has to be late dusk. He settles in, nearly invisible, where he can overlook the marsh, and starts to bob in place. We hear his "peent" calls, over and over again. Then, abruptly, he takes off on a spiraling flight, high overhead, before dropping back down again. His feathers make soft tinkly sounds as he returns to his starting ground. Again, and again—every night throughout April and May—he sings and soars, until something tells him enough is enough.

Some people think that humans, who are not limited to DNA-based knowledge, are the smartest of animals. I am not so sure. When I observe creatures who are more closely linked to genetic wisdom, I don't feel so smart. For instance, starting in April I watch the deluge of long distance migrators, impressed with how these birds know how to find their way back to breeding grounds every year. I marvel at the tiny hummingbirds who regularly come back from Mexico looking for our feeders during the first week in May. To accomplish such a journey they must rely on all kinds of wisdom from body-based senses that I lack.

Even those who just stop to rest are already focused on sex. On a sunny day two mallard pairs dozing on a mini-island of reeds in the nearest beaver pond catch my attention. One male wakes, stretches, and slips quietly into the water, bobbing his head, inviting his mate to join him. The second drake wakes and accosts the pair, bothering the female until she flies off. Then he chases the other male up onto nearby ice. The hullabaloo wakes a sleeping female, who moves decisively toward the aggressive male. When she bobs her head at him, he forgets his fury and docilely follows her around the pond.

I watch, bemused. I know how to be a peacemaker too, but not because I have had to keep Sandy from chasing other women. Neither of us grew up in families that dealt well with anger, and we both have trouble expressing dark emotions and reacting to them. Mimicking my parents' discomfort with anger, my first response is to squelch the flames, while Sandy keeps his feelings close to his heart.

After fifteen years here, when we rub each other the wrong way, first come snide remarks that speak of hidden anger. Then, one or both of us erupt. Afterward, we each go our own way, turning to the Valley as peacemaker. Irritations dwindle in the sun as Sandy communes with a grouse taking a dust bath in the road, and I notice an unfamiliar snake. We rush back to share our sightings, our dissension forgotten.

Learning to deal with the anger I direct at myself has been more difficult. I wish I could emulate the kingfisher I observe at the beaver pond. While he sounds very aggressive as he roars around, noisily announcing his presence, he soon becomes the picture of patience. Perched quietly on a stump, he vigilantly peruses the water around him. Fifteen minutes later when I am ready to leave, he is still intent on fishing. Before I can move, he dives and erupts out of the water with a fish twice his size dangling from his beak. Without any apparent qualms about how he will ingest the big fish, he methodically bangs it against a tree branch—first to the right, then to the left—breaking all its bones. He then flies off to join his mate high in a pine, where they feast on fish. He knows just what he needs to do, and I admire his perseverance.

Unlike the kingfisher, I live a quiet life for the most part. It is only when I can't figure out how to do something that I erupt in frustration. I glare at the broken sink sprayer that has sprung a leak. Anger curls up inside me as I stare at the darn thing, knowing I will never be able to figure out how it is supposed to work. My knee-jerk reaction holds me hostage to believing that I am no good at tinkering. And, of course, I can't tinker with all that anger boiling inside. Sandy shakes his head at my fit, and figures out that we need a new sprayer. Once I calm down, I can see that he is like the kingfisher, successful because he is so confident and patient. And I benefit, just like the kingfisher's mate.

Certainly Sandy has benefited from some of my traits. He knows that he can count on my doing what I say I am going to do and that I am happy to share the chores that make living at Journey's End possible. My willingness to wear the diplomat's hat has resulted in our living more tranquil lives than we might have otherwise. When our children were young he depended on my patience as a parent. I think I can hold my own with the twenty-seven species of birds we have observed raising families here, but who's to say how well I would manage if I gave birth to a flock of babies every year. Three children in four years demanded all my energy and ingenuity.

Birds as devoted caregivers to the next generation surround us on summer days. We never know whom we may see. On one walk I watch a yellow-bellied sapsucker carry off a sack of chick poop from its nest hole in a snag. Left behind are young who squawk furiously. Tramping along the road through the wetlands, we spy least flycatcher, red-eyed vireo, evening grosbeak, rose-breasted grosbeak, and yellowthroat parents feeding their young. While Sandy watches from the kitchen window, mama woodcock brings her seven chicks to a nearby wet spot where she instructs them in worm hunting. The next day, I observe an ovenbird limp off into the woods, and discover his mate and their brood hidden inside an oven-shaped nest in tall grass.

Then there are the inconstant tree swallows who arrive in May to fight over our four bird houses. They compete aggressively, knocking each other out of the sky, until things are settled. Then they switch to picking up nesting materials and copulating on nearby tree branches. Even with all the shenanigans, some of the couples are so flighty that they don't settle down in their hard-earned houses, deciding to skip child rearing, at least here.

If I put aside my fear of heights, I can see myself as a swallow, whooping it up in the sky (if not having sex in a tree). While their zooming flights hustling after insects are probably all work, they seem to be having fun: flying, diving, and performing dipping maneuvers in the air. Watching how effortlessly they appear to live, I feel my wings spreading. As I imagine becoming a swallow, I realize that my fears of what will happen when this body of mine dies no longer stifle me at night. I am just one more bit of evolving life.

Watching a colony of blue herons who raise their young in a rookery gives us front-row seats to transformation. We find them, just a bushwhack off the road along Tongue Mountain's ridge. In April we hear the herons before we see them: guttural grunts, squawks, and raucous calls fill the air above the silver shimmer of the beaver pond where twenty branchy nests perch high in dead trees. Several are condo-trees with six or seven nests stacked along trunks, apartments that are all balcony. We watch open-mouthed as the herons interact—greeting each other with calls reminiscent of hinges badly in need of oil, undertaking noisy chases, and copulating—a precarious business when these tall birds get romantic on a tree branch.

Return visits display heron metamorphosis right before our eyes and ears. In May, we watch lone adults brood three to five eggs. After the chicks hatch, our birding scope reveals whitish, fuzzy baby heads bobbing in nests with an adult close by. In two weeks, the babies become ravenous, and their "kak-kakk-kak" calls welcome Mom or Dad's return with food. By mid-June, the youngsters jostle and poke one another, wrestling for their returning parent's proffered beak-full of partly digested frogs or fish.

One nest is a worry, for the babies don't seem to grow. Weeks later I realize with horror that they are stuck in the nest, apparently having lost their parents. Then the young birds disappear, perhaps becoming the hawk that shows up one day, leering from one branch of a dead tree while an adolescent heron teeters on another. I can believe that mortality is high in this first year, as the new generation tries to figure out how to fly and find a way down to the meals waiting in the pond.

The risks of raising young in the wild are stunning. We haven't always been helpful even though we have the best of intentions. The phone aerial on the front porch scared off a pair of barn swallows who had tried to settle next to it; they couldn't deal with this neighbor who kept moving as we tried to get better reception. Then there was a robin mother who was dive-bombed by blue jays, day after day, in her nest high in a tall white pine, out of reach of any help I could give.

Squirrels and chipmunks raid nests, seeking eggy nourishment, while cowbird females aim to add their large eggs to broods of eggs laid by other mothers. Abhorring this parasitic behavior, we sought to discourage the cowbirds. When stones from slingshots failed to connect, Sandy borrowed a BB gun and managed to shoot two birds before he realized that doing this was every bit as dreadful as the bird behavior. So he stopped.

We try to leave rescues to bird parents, but thrill when we get peeks at new behaviors. An adult robin hops across the lawn, followed by a youngster. I guess that Papa is leading the way. Hop, hop, hop—goes dad; hop, hop, hop—goes son, peeping an occasional piteous cry. He gets a worm pushed down his throat, and they hop again. Soon I see baby digging at the ground with his beak, and the birds dance a twosome—hippity hop, parent first, child next, learning the ways of robin life. These bird babies remind me how much I miss our two grandchildren, who live nine hours away in Cleveland; much too distant for frequent dances with us.

Much as I long to see them, I am thankful that we live in Wardboro Valley; that we made the changes necessary to allow us to observe and reflect on all we've seen, heard, smelled, and touched here. It seems we are in the right place, at the right time. There is nothing I would rather do than watch the fireflies, whom I observe on a June night. In every direction their flashes light up the dark, as they flit their sex dance. Males flash high, females low. Their lights lead each other to breed and produce the next generation.

As I sit in the dark, astounded by the light show, I realize how much there is to marvel at here. How can a monarch be related to a caterpillar or chrysalis? How can there be an oak tree inside an acorn, or an apple inside a blossom? I have read that mammals—whether human, coyote, bat, rabbit, or mouse—have early embryos that seem almost identical with one another. Yet most of the time we act as if the others are not like us at all. In fact, we are all brothers and sisters under the skin. I mourn when we feel forced to snuff out mouse or chipmunk lives. Who are we killing but ourselves?

In August, when I walk through a field and find a striped monarch caterpillar on a milkweed plant devouring its leaves, I wonder what it must be like to do nothing but eat. What must it be like to fold into a chrysalis, and rest, before emerging with wings ready to fly beyond the asters toward Mexico?

On September 1, 2001, I find one chrysalis dangling from the front porch banister. This apparent light green ornament with gold filigree hangs from a black thread. I hover, worrying that this butterfly will hatch too late to make its trip south successfully. Habitat changes made by human beings along their flyway have made their journey increasingly difficult. Then, too, many died during severe cold spells at their Mexican winter home in recent years. Six days later, when I step onto the porch at 7:20 on a chilly fifty-degree morning, the chrysalis is gone. Instead, nearby on a peony leaf, a monarch lies with folded wings. Within hours, the butterfly is gone.

On September 11, I am relieved. I believe the hummingbirds and butterflies have moved on toward Mexico. Sandy chops wood. I pull up dead cucumber vines and broadfork one garden plot, refreshed by the cool air and bright sunshine. It is a good day to be alive. Although we know nothing about it in our television-less home, two hundred miles to the south, death and destruction rock New York City. We learn about the crumbling towers only when the phone rings as we eat lunch, and hear our daughter Bonnie's anxious voice. She relays the horrifying news.

We drift to chores to keep our bodies busy. This usually quiet place is even quieter without the frequent drone of airplanes passing overhead.

Sandy calls me to look at a peculiar toad he has found.

"I think it has only one back leg."

We stare at the toad, jolted. The natural world seems to be going crazy, too. I shudder to think we might have somehow poisoned him. Even if we didn't harm the toad, the impact of human technology could have damaged life, even here in this seemingly out-of-the-way place. For, indeed, we are tied to everywhere else.

To deal with the violent waste of life, it helps to center ourselves in the ongoing nature of this Valley: to watch the sun rising above Catamount Mountain, to follow the cloud formations rolling by overhead, and to meditate on Catamount's fiery glow at sunset when dusk swaths us. Or to look skyward in the nearly complete darkness of a Valley night and see the approach of the constellation Orion, knowing that by New Year's it will be right overhead. I am reassured that life will go on, regardless of what we humans do to one another and the environment.

But just the same, I am reminded how fleeting individual lives are. I don't usually notice changes in myself, until I look in the mirror and find more white hairs, or recognize some aches that have become an unpleasant part of my body sense. Visits by our children always shake me up. It seems as though they have hardly arrived when it is time for good-byes. As I hug them, I wish I could hold them here and stop the clock. It's hard to believe that once upon a time they were helpless and dependent on us. Some day we may be dependent on them.

We are struggling to cope with the deaths of Nora and Marc Merrill. When these neighbors passed on, they left a big hole in our Valley connections. We attempt to emulate them, and enjoy each moment. They always kept track of passersby who might need help. Marc relished telling how they rescued lost hunters, helped wandering children find their parents, and lost dogs find their owners. We follow this tradition, shuttling hunters back to the other side of Catamount, and returning stray beagles to their owners miles away in Horicon.

Unexpectedly, one April morning, I find a refugee who needs a home. Driving along the quiet road, I come upon a beagle-like dog running with his nose to the ground. Frightened by the car, he veers off into the woods and then climbs a bank where he watches me. I stop the car, and speak softly to him before slowly moving into the trees, up the bank toward him. He wags his tail and rolls over. This dirty, skinny guy has no collar. His head is a mix of black and brown, and the rest of his white body is spotted, with large black splashes on his torso, and brown dribbles on his legs. His eyes seem so soft and beseeching.

"Come on," I urge, and walk back toward the car. He trots next to me, jumping inside the car after I open the door. Once I get in, he pushes close and slinks into my lap with a big sigh. When no one comes looking for a lost dog, we figure he belongs here. We name him Ward. Within days of his arrival he confronts a porcupine and returns with his nose full of quills. Within a few weeks, he follows a coyote up the hill behind the house and joins in some kind of feed, returning with a sick stomach.

His nose and ears beat ours any day. We marvel at him when he punctures a quiet evening in front of the fire with howls as he responds to coyotes we can't hear. He follows his nose on adventures that leave us behind. He has invaded our hearts. After three years of being a Wardboro dog, I think he calls Journey's End home, too. He has become goofy over Sandy and will sit in his lap for hours, if invited. He centers our lives, giving us a new understanding of just how empowering love can be.

I like to think the passion and caring of love burns invisibly, but powerfully. I can see flashes of it when Ward gets silly and tears around the yard just out of reach; doing a loop-the-loop that includes both maple trees and Sandy's parents' ashes. Just as surely as the fire transforms logs in my stove, love has flamed in us, altering us too. Ward may have been one spark, but the wild creatures we have come to know in Wardboro have also made us more caring people, who agonize over the times we have felt forced to end lives in order to make our home here.

We reflect on the message from the memorial service so many years ago that spurred us to move here and entwine our lives with that of Wardboro Valley. We may be dying a little every day, but along the way we rejoice in the way our lives have been transformed by the Valley whose spirit never dies. We find it increasingly difficult to define where it ends and we begin.

Just like Wardboro's farmers, some day we will leave Journey's End, and once we do, I imagine our impact here will gradually disappear. On the other hand, we are not the travelers who arrived here too early one spring. When we move on, we will do so as different beings. No longer do I fear the death of my body that I know awaits. Life has poured into me and will someday pour out. Once my turn to hold time is over, I anticipate returning here as ashes sprinkled by my family. But now, I cherish living between the two pourings.

Two great blue herons atop a dead tree, each preening its body feathers intently, before shifting to preen each other. Perhaps it's the male who then catches his mate's neck in his beak with a gentle embrace. All the while they brace against a hefty breeze that threatens to blow them off their perch. At their feet rests a miscellany of branches and sticks—a nest in the making. The male flies off and returns with a stick, landing next to his companion, who arches her head and bows low before him. She takes the stick and pokes it into the nest, with the male's beak acting as a rudder. Off he flies again, returning with a longer, unwieldy branch that both birds grab and manipulate until it blends into the nest too.

"How can they do all this using only their beaks?" I whisper, scarcely breathing. The intimacy of the herons at work—their devotion to each other and their everyday challenges—gives me goose bumps. I grab Sandy's hand and hold on.